THE CEMENT BENCH

The JOURNEY of one woman's survival of
an emotionally abusive relationship with a
Sociopathic Narcissist to her FREEDOM
and Living with a Life of SOUL.

By Mary A. Faher

Disclaimers: I have changed the name of everyone involved to protect their privacy and to protect me from any legal issues. I did not use the name of the financial institution that I worked for; however, I really wanted to.

Table of Contents

DEDICATION

To my wonderful friends: Jan Johnson, Fran Miller, Ginny Goodenough, Jennifer Glaser, and Debbie Goodsell:

What a Blessed woman I am to have such support and love from each of you, which have sustained me during the darkest of times and have been there when my will to survive was low and my very will to live was at stake. I can never thank you enough for being true friends. The Creator has sent each of you, my angels. I love you!

To my wonderful son, Ian: I am so blessed that you chose me as your mother. You have been so supporting and accepting of me at a time when I questioned, even my own sanity. Your Love has been never ending and I know that I can always count on you to be here for me. My Love for you is today, tomorrow and eternally.

To Kathryn Kirkdorfer, thank you for helping me to see that a book is more than just what has happened and words. It is about the journey, about digging deeper to bring clarity to the reader and shedding light on the dark places so that the healing can continue.

To you, the reader of The Cement Bench: I am so honored to have you share a piece of my JOURNEY. It has been a privilege to share such a deep heart-tearing subject, knowing that you might still be healing from your own JOURNEY and that I might in some way be instrumental in that healing process.

Well, I've been afraid of changing
'cause I've built my life
Around you...
But time makes you bolder
Children get older...
And I'm getting older, too
Yes, I'm getting older too...

*-   Stevie Nicks * Landslide*

Great way to start the year off!

What a great way to start the new year off, Happy New Year 2011, in the holding tank of the Berrien County Jail. The light was bright and illuminated the approximately 12x12 cement block cell with only a stainless steel sink/toilet combo, a payphone and of course a cement bench, cement everywhere, iron bars on the door. The only sound was the large woman lying on the cement floor, taking up about half of the area, snoring and with every exhale of breath reeked the smell of alcohol. She had not even stirred as I was led into the room, dazed, stunned at my new surroundings. It was hard to judge time, what was time; it certainly wasn't anything in there. It was as if time had stopped and that I was just going through the motions of living. Sometime later, I heard the matron ushering a new occupant to the cell next to ours. How many were in here? How many were allowed in each cell? I kept asking myself; HOW DID I GET HERE?

After finally laying flat on the cement bench, still wearing the clothes that I had meticulously adorned for work almost 24 hours before, I heard keys rattling, there was a clanking as the door opened and a young woman was led in. Clank…it was locked and I sat up, the woman on the floor didn't move and it was obvious that she was sleeping something off. By this time the obnoxious odor was gone or I had become accustomed to it. I slid over to the corner so the wall could help prop me up. We smiled at each other as a sign of recognition. "You don't look like you belong here" she said, "What are you in for?" As the words came out of my mouth, it was as if someone else was speaking, "Attempted murder", I said…"Oooh", she said smiling as to give me some sort of recognition, as if that was an honorable thing. Silence, a minute or two later she asked, "If you don't mind me asking, what exactly did you do? You don't look the type." I asked myself, what is the type? I am a white 53 year old woman who is dressed in a brown suit, makeup and hair done sitting on a cement bench. What does an attempted murderess look like? I heard words coming out of my mouth, but it was as if someone else was speaking. "I stabbed my husband". Laughter, there was laughter coming out of the young woman. "You should have killed him then," more laughter.

I might have smiled, I am not really sure, I couldn't feel my face. "If I had wanted the bastard dead, I would have killed him, you can be sure of that", I added.

"What are you in here for?" I looked at her as she spoke, such a young pretty girl, with perfect eyebrows, I learned later that she did them herself; she had learned to do the thread method when she had been in jail the time before. She offered to do mine when we got out. I learned that she had violated her probation by not making the fine payments, that she was currently living in Detroit with her mother and her son. She had gone to the county jail there to make a payment and they arrested her. They had driven her to this county where she had been originally booked and charged. I asked "What was your crime?" She laughed at me, said the way I talked was so formal. She had been caught with prescription drugs that weren't hers; she had bought Valium on the street. She didn't sell it; it was for her personal use. She had already served some time and was on probation. She started to cry about her son when she started to talk about leaving him with her mother, she didn't get even to say goodbye, because she didn't know she would be arrested. She was trying to get her life turned around, she was off of drugs, but because of her record, she said, couldn't get work. She had been getting assistance for her son and if it weren't for her mother, they would be out on the street. I asked about the boy's father and she just laughed and said "That's a joke, he's a joke!" I left it at that, I was feeling so drained, I didn't need to know everything about my new found cell mate.

A while later the keys rattled, the door clanked, the door opened and in walked another young woman. I had to change my position on the cement bench from sitting "Indian" style to just sitting up to accommodate the third person on the bench. She was a slight gal, I bet she didn't weigh 100 pounds and she looked stunned and in a daze. She sat down and put her head on her lap without saying a word. We sat there in silence listening to the snoring woman on the floor. I tried closing my eyes, the bright light, again asking myself HOW WAS IT THAT I WAS HERE?

I could hear a little more activity, keys rattling, door clanking and in came another young woman. She didn't look at all dazed to be here, I thought to myself, she has been here before and I later learned that, that was the case. She had those long fake

4

fingernails, long fake eyelashes, a weave very artfully done, her makeup was meticulous, and actually she was very beautiful. The three of us introduced ourselves and the other two just kept sleeping. I was waiting for her to ask what I was in for; I was ready this time and waited to see her reaction. "Oh girl, you should have killed him!" I came back with my pat answer, I was sticking to that. I learned that she had been arrested because her employer had said she had stolen from him and she of course denied it. Said they were just setting her up and her boyfriend, who was in law enforcement, would be by in the morning with her bail money.

We could hear more stirring as others were led to other cells. How many are there here? Again, I asked myself WHAT HAS BROUGHT ME TO THIS? Our cell was opened yet again, the young woman sat on the floor and it brought the large woman to finally sit up. She stretched and slowly smiled. She actually was a lot younger than I thought. She had a beautiful smile, her tongue was pierced, and she must have been 6 ft. tall. She was a big woman and gave off the vibes of DON'T MESS WITH ME and nobody did. We all had to rearrange ourselves as she walked over to the toilet, looked up at the camera that I had not even noticed and gave it the finger knowing that the guards were watching. I wanted to laugh but thought better of it. She sat down and let it rip. She apologized; the toilet was actually the only real seat in the room besides the cement bench. The phone is right next to the toilet, so she sat there and tried calling her sister. You have to call collect and it took her about eight tries before her sister would accept the charges. She was swearing and yelling at her sister to get the fucking bond money. Then the crying came, how was her son? More swearing, more yelling and with that her sister hung up on her. Next she tried calling her mother, but her mother wouldn't accept any of the calls. This must have gone on for over an hour. Others inmates were yelling from other cells for her to quiet down. Things were stirring up now.

Two more women were added to our group. I asked God, how many will they put in here? After introductions there was always the question of what are you in for and always amazement that I was there. I have to say, that being an attempted murderess gave me some status. I could tell no one was going to mess with

5

me!

I told the large woman that I thought she looked like she was a Samoan. She said that she got that a lot but that she was half black and half white. She was in for domestic violence against her partner; they had been drinking and doing their laundry at the local Laundromat. She went on to call her all of the names she could think of, most I wouldn't put in writing. She was never going back to her, etc.

More noise, the trustee was bringing the breakfast cart. Someone said, "Better eat the breakfast; it will be the best meal of the day". The day, I was stunned to think that I might be there a whole day. I wasn't going to be there a whole day, someone was going to finally ask me about this and I could explain and go home. After breakfast I would get this straightened out. I wasn't hungry and passed the tray around and it was eaten. What time was it? There wasn't a clock, none of us had a watch on, and again time was just suspended.

Hours earlier when I was booked, I had to take off all of my jewelry and my watch and put them in a small paper bag as well as my nylons and high heels, cell phone, suit coat and purse. I signed my name on the bag and the matron put it in a locker. She asked me a series of questions; I don't even remember half of what I told her. She talked to the Township Police officer and I heard him say Attempted Murder! Attempted Murder? Are they talking about me? Again, I asked myself WHAT AM I DOING HERE? She then led me to a room and had me take all of my clothes off and stand in front of her as she searched my mouth, body and even had me turn around, bend over and grunt. Grunt of all things. She then gave me my clothes back and a pair of sandals that didn't fit well, my feet are wide so I had to wear a few sizes too big. She led me to a hallway that led to a room that was used for finger printing and mug shots. I had been finger printed several times before in my life, all for my position in the financial industry. It always had consisted of the black ink pad and using an orange soap to get it off. Times had changed, now with the digital age of the computer, I rolled my fingers and there were the

6

prints. The machine told the Matron that it was clear.
I remember standing against the wall for the mug shots. I
COULDN'T BELIEVE IT WAS HAPPENING!!! It was
like being in a movie and no one had asked me to star in it!
As we left the room, I got to see my "mug" shot, that was
me? I looked like a crazy woman, the eyes said it all!
Oh My God, was I crazy?

It was obvious that everyone in here knew the ropes; they had all been in jail before. It was like they were all playing their role as an inmate. But me, WHAT WAS I DOING HERE? Someone in the group asked me what my bond was going to be? I must have had a blank stare on my face because someone spoke up for me; they all seemed to know that this was my first time behind bars. They were debating whether it was going to be $50,000 or even $100,000. "Are you going to be able to come up with the money?" Someone asked and I must have just stared. "Well, she can call Bovo if she needs to," someone chimed in. Bovo? Who and what was Bovo? I learned that Bovo was the name of the local Bond Bailsman located across the street from the jail. You could hire him by paying part of the bond and he would put up the rest, for a fee. If you broke the conditions of the bond, he got to keep the upfront money and still try to collect on the rest.

I kept thinking WHEN was someone going to come and get me out? Oh My God, no one had even missed me! Surely someone from work would notice I wasn't there! But who would they call? Miguel, my husband, wouldn't be home, he had just started a new job. As I sat there, listening to my cell mates, who by this time numbered ten, talking on the phone to family, friends, and Bovo, it occurred to me that I hadn't had my one free phone call. I went to the door and looked for the trustee. I waited until she walked by and said "Excuse me, excuse me". "Are you talking to me?" she replied coldly. "Do you think I am just here to wait on you hand and foot? What do you want?" "I didn't get my free phone call and wondered if I could do that now?" I could hear the laughter behind me and the slow smile on the trustee's face. "That's only on TV that you get a free phone call, in here you have to use the pay phone." She then proceeded to walk away.

I walked to my seat on the cement bench, this time I was on

the edge, towards the door, sitting next to the young girl that was still sleeping with her head on her lap. She hadn't even woken up for breakfast. Ok, so no free phone-call, who am I going to call? Not my son, he was away at college and if I could, I didn't want him to know about this. Who else? I must have sat there for an hour, I don't know, because time had ceased to exist. I couldn't think. Everyone was so loud. I was tired, but I knew I couldn't sleep. I hadn't been sleeping well at home for at least two years. Think Mary, who can you call? The only person I could think of was a friend named Gail, she didn't work outside of the home, and she would be home. So, there was someone I could call; only problem, I didn't know her phone number. It was on my cell phone and I just pushed a button. I didn't know anyone's number. Truth be told, even if I had, I am sure I wouldn't have been able to recall it. Again, asking myself WHAT AM I GOING TO DO? I asked someone if we could dial an operator to look up a number and that was quickly answered: NO.

I heard the Matron yelling "FAHER!" I quickly got up and went to the door. There was a woman there with an order from the court that I take the DNA test. She informed me that if I didn't, I would be in violation and that was an offense I would be charged with also. A DNA test! What was next? I remember opening my mouth and as she swabbed the inside, I thought to myself that now my DNA was going to be officially kept somewhere, by someone. My mind raced, well at least when they find my decaying body somewhere, they will be able to identify me.

I walked back to the cell door and waited for the trustee to come back by. It looked like she was busy, but I finally got her attention, she frowned at me. "What now" "I need to make a phone call and the number is on my cell phone, could I get that?" "There's no way you are going to get your phone." "Well, is there a phone book I can see?" I asked. "You don't ask for much, do you? You can't use the phone book, but when I am not busy, I can look a number up for you, I'll be back later." So I went and sat down. The girl next to me finally stirred. She sat up and just stared. Someone asked her what she was in for. In a very timid voice she said that her boyfriend and she had robbed a couple of gas stations. That they didn't have any money for food and knew that the gasoline companies were rich; they didn't want to hurt anybody. They had gotten away with robbing one and got caught on the second one. I learned later that her four year old son was in the back seat of the car and had been taken into protective child services. They had gone on a robbing spree with her son in the back seat!

"FAHER!" It was the trustee, she called me to the cell door and gave me a piece of paper and pencil and said "Write the name you want me to look up". I did, I gave it to her and returned to my seat. A few minutes later she came back with the number on the piece of paper. She said, "You might want to keep this, in case you need it again." I thanked her.

I sat on the cold stainless steel toilet as I dialed the number and noticed that my hands were shaking, making it difficult to push the correct number. Finally in what seemed like an eternity, the phone was ringing! The automatic operator came on and said that the party had not accepted the collect call charges. If I wished to make the call again, please hang up and dial again. My hands were shaking as I dialed the number again, surely Gail would accept my call! Again, the same message, the party had not accepted the collect call charges. I remember my mind asking again, WHAT AM I DOING HERE, WHAT AM I GOING TO DO?

What's next, I hated not knowing what to expect, what time was it? Did anybody know that I was here? Shivers went down my spine, I was cold, it was cold in there. I wouldn't get my thyroid medication that day and I had missed a day before. I could take it tomorrow when I got home, I remember telling myself. I think I had blocked some of the noise out, but I tuned back in when I heard them talking about the bitch, which bitch? The jail, that is what they called it, the bitch, the prosecutor was the bitch, the guard was the bitch, I had to laugh, I had never heard so much swearing and I came from a family of swearing as the norm. I learned that we were going to see a judge about our arraignment and he would set our bail. That started at 2:00. We would all be led down to a room and wait for our turn.

Somebody was talking to me, I must have spaced out. Plead not guilty, don't ever plead guilty, make them prove it; make them prove you did what they say you did. Hopefully you won't get that Fucker Judge Willie; he hates everyone and if you get him, ask for another judge. Who's your attorney? Questions, questions,

9

questions and more questions. The voice inside was asking, WHY AM I HERE? Oh Gail, please answer the phone!

I made my way over the toilet, sat down and dialed the numbers on the paper for Gail; I can hear it ringing….Hello? Gail, it's me, it's Mary! Oh My God you answered the phone! She answered by saying "I decided that it must be someone I knew that was in trouble and I had better accept the charges, I never dreamed it would be you! The operator said will you accept a collect call from Berrien County Jail. I thought it was a joke!" I immediately said, Gail, you know I will repay you for everything! Listen, this call is timed and I am in jail for attempted murder of Miguel, I stabbed him. I am going to see the judge this afternoon and he will set my bail, please call attorney B., he is the attorney I want. I will call you back when I know what my bail is and Gail, I can't believe that I am in here. Please call the financial institution that I work for at their South Street branch, let them know that I will be out of touch for a couple of days and then call Ian and let him know I am safe and that I will call him when I can. Oh My God Gail, I can't believe this. I Love you…bye.

I couldn't believe it, what if Gail hadn't accepted the phone call? She didn't know it was from me! My brain was on overload with what had happened in the last 24 hours with no sleep. All of a sudden I felt tired, like I could sleep. With ten women in the cell, there wasn't any place you could spread out and it was so cold in there. One of the women had a mat to lay or sit on. She was pregnant and they gave pregnant women mats. She was a doll and shared it. I laid down on the floor with my head on someone's leg for a pillow, we were all bunched together to stay warm. Someone laughed saying we should be glad that we were women, we didn't mind lying together, the men were probably freezing, afraid to touch each other. That did bring a smile to my face. Men, what pigs I thought!

I slept and it must have been a deep sleep, I didn't hear the women getting up to get their lunch tray. I got up to get mine and it was true, I should have had breakfast, this looked awful. I was a vegetarian at that time and the goulash didn't look appetizing. There were green beans and an apple and a cookie in a package. I drank the juice and saved the apple and ate the green beans, I gave away the rest. One of the women said that if I wasn't going to eat the apple to hide it, we weren't allowed to save things. Now where was I going to hide an apple? I thought to myself. So I ended up giving it away.

Just as we were getting settled into positions that everyone could live with, we heard the rattling of the keys, the clank of the door and in came in yet another woman. That brought our number to eleven. How many were they going to put in here? Introductions went around the room. Her story was that she was on leave from the army and was taking a vacation with her children and was arrested for not paying off a court fee from a few years ago. She said she wasn't worried, the Army would get her out ASAP because they needed her. She said they would be able to take priority over the legal system. Who was I, she could be right. The noise volume was so loud; I really can't/couldn't tolerate noise at such a level for such a long time. In fact as far back as I can remember I never could tolerate noise or crowds for any length of time.

The trustee came by and gave everyone a sheet of paper and one pencil that we passed around. It was a questionnaire about if we worked, how much money we made, were we able to hire an attorney or should one be appointed to us. A little time later, it must have been around 2:00 because our door opened, we were asked to line up to go to see the judge. Finally, I could tell someone my side of what happened and make this go away. We were instructed not to talk to anyone on the way, and that we would go through the men's section. Evidently they were having a problem with one of the men defecating all over his cell and it reeked the place up. We were silent, and as we walked through the hallway of the men's cells, I could feel their eyes follow us as we made our way through. We were led to a holding room and waited our turn. Two at a time were taken in and I was prepared, the women had told me that I would sit in front of a TV monitor, the judge would be in another room, would ask questions. That was exactly what happened. He was reading what the prosecutor had recommended and he had the ability to go with that or make his own decisions. He said in light of the fact that this was my first offense; he thought the recommendations were a little harsh, none the less, that is was what he was going to go with. $25,000.00 bail, I was to be tethered to home until I came back next week for my hearing with the assigned judge…The Honorable Judge Willie. Oh My God, didn't the women warn me about him? Wasn't anybody going to ask me anything, about what happened? I remember being stunned, dazed, again. Where was my voice?

As we walked back to our cell, everyone was quiet. I have to admit I was in a world of my own. What had just happened? The cell had been cleaned out by the trustee while we were gone. It does get messy when you have so many women in such a little space. I noticed that the other cells looked full with the exception of one, in that one there appeared to be only one woman.

When we were all in and locked down, immediately there was jockeying for the telephone. The phone wasn't working; we found out that when inmates are being moved from one area to another, the phones are shut off. One of the women got the attention of the Trustee and asked her to have the phone put back on. After a while, someone tried the phone and again, it was still down. The Samoan was not having it, she pushed the red button that was located above the toilet and it clearly stated: FOR EMERGENCY ONLY, she told the guard that the phone was not working and needed to be turned back on. The guard said he would take care of that and reminded her that the button was for emergencies only. She tried to explain to him that we had a cell filled with women that needed to make calls. Nothing was happening, people kept trying the phone and of course there was yelling, drama, I could feel myself withdrawing. The Trustee came by and said we had "pissed off the guards" and they weren't going to turn the phone on until they felt like it. They wanted to teach us a lesson about using the button. After what seemed like another hour, one of the women asked to see the Matron. She came to the door and the Samoan explained the situation and said that the whole cell shouldn't be punished because the guard and she had had words. The Matron said she would see what she could do. A few minutes later the Samoan tried the phone and it worked, she called her mother, she called her sister, she called her lover and no one had the money for the bail. I think she needed $900.00 which was 10% of the $9,000 bond. She was mad, very mad and got louder as it all went down. The other cell mates were getting anxious; they wanted their turn to call for bond money. The trustee came to the door and asked the Samoan to step outside.

I wondered if she was going to be told to be a little quieter. Another woman was on the phone to Bovo, the Bondsman. It was finally my turn, I called Gail, and she answered the phone, what a relief. I told her that my bond was set at $25,000.00, however, I only needed $2,500.00 (10% of the bond) to be bailed out and $100.00 deposit for the tether machine to be set up. Both of it had to be separate, because they went to different departments. She told me that she had contacted the lawyer, and that attorney B. was in Florida, but his associate Mr. M. would be able to take the case. She told me not to say on the phone or to anyone, what had happened, that everything was being taped. I sighed with relief, finally, and then the news, "Mary, you are going to have to spend the night again, the tether office closes at 2:00 p.m. each day." ANOTHER night here? Oh My God, Oh My God! You have to be joking? I knew that Gail wouldn't joke about that. She was trying to be encouraging; she told me she had left a message at the financial institution that I worked for and had let my son know that I was OK and not to worry. I thought, WHEN IS THIS NIGHTMARE GOING TO END?

I was back once again, on the cement bench, in my favorite position next to the wall. The trustee came to the door and slid the yellow papers to everyone with the information about their bond, assigned judge, time and date of next court appearance, etc. When I got mine, all I saw was ATTEMPTED MURDER and Judge Willie. The cell was like a hive of bees, everyone wanted to know what everybody got and which judge and when it came to be my turn, they got quiet. Up to that point $9000.00 was the highest bond; even so, they weren't surprised that mine was $25,000.00. The pretty woman with the long fake nails was called to the door, her boyfriend had posted bail, and she was getting out! I know we all envied her, she had called it, she said her boyfriend would pay the minute he knew what the amount was. We wished her well and she wished us all well.

The Samoan was brought back and she didn't say anything at first, so I was the one to ask her what they wanted with her. She said the Bitch wanted her to rat out someone so she could get her bond lowered, if she cooperated. She was a city cab driver and it seems, knew people. She said there was no way she was going to do that! It would mean death to her and there was no way she was

13

going to do that. So she went back on the toilet seat, making Phone-calls, was anybody going to help get her out? I learned that a bondsman would only bail you out if you paid part of the bail to him, she was looking for someone to do that. The crying that went on, she was crying over the fact that it was her son's birthday and she was going to miss it. Oh the noise, the nagging voice... WHAT AM I DOING HERE? A couple more women were released after their bonds were paid. Not me, I was going to spend another night in jail. I just couldn't believe it. I was cold, I was achy, and I was exhausted. I needed my meds; I could feel it in my joints. I felt dirty and I wanted to go home.

The trustee came around and dropped off paper bags with our dinner in them. A sandwich, with an orange, celery/carrot in a plastic bag. And a box of raisins. I learned that at night, dinner was always a brown bag event. That way the county didn't have to pay for help to clean up after dinner...whatever. I could feel myself starting to shut down, it was more than just not having my meds, I was emotionally shutting down, this had been too much.

The Samoan was starting to get testy; she wanted out and wanted out now. She kept calling her mother, her sister, her lover and making everyone tense in the cell, finally I looked her in the face and said "You don't scare me, I know that inside you, is just a big marshmallow, you might fool most of the people but I have your number!" With that I smiled and she smiled. In that moment in time, we were connected; two sisters who understood that each of us had gone through a lot of darkness and had survived. Each of us had taken a different path on the journey...but we knew that we shared some commonality and that had led to our meeting on this path at this time of our lives.

A couple of the women had bonded out leaving a little more room. Just about the time I thought I could stretch out another young woman was added to our group. She looked to be in her early twenties and of course there were the standard greetings and what are you in for. She surprised me when she said that she had beat up her boyfriend. She added that when he had beat her up, she hadn't called the police on him. So she was just another woman in here for domestic violence. Actually, half of the group was in here for that. I found that interesting. Once again, I heard the keys rattle; the door clanked and in walked a woman

14

looking to be closer to my age. She introduced herself, the usual greetings etc. and as it turned out, she was in for writing bad checks. It was her second offense. She just seemed to laugh it off. She told of how she had hid out in a friend's trailer and that a policeman had come to the door and the friend let him in. That was how she got caught. Then she admitted she had smoked some weed before coming in. I wondered how many had been using drugs before they were in here.

Finally it was time the Samoan got to leave. The matron came and told her she had been bonded and she just beamed that gorgeous smile and told everybody goodbye, stopped and smiled at me and said, good luck! With that, my first cell mate was gone. It was quite a group as I think about it…domestic violence, bad check writing, breaking bond, robbing gas stations, and of course, my attempted murder. I was hoping it was going to be an uneventful evening, but something told me that wasn't going to happen the way I would have liked.

The woman that was in for writing bad checks was asking the trustee to check on the nurse to see when she was going to get her meds. She had a pacemaker and took something to alleviate water build up and she wanted her meds. She wanted them now. She looked uncomfortable, I didn't know if it was because she needed her meds or the high was finally wearing off.

By this time, I was back on the cement bench, trying to get comfortable, knowing that I probably was going to try to sleep sitting up. The young woman that was in for DV was talking about her family life, of abandonment, abuse, drug use. She had been diagnosed as bi-polar and had seizures. She said she felt like she was going to have a seizure. The woman closest to the door called for the trustee. The trustee room was exactly across the hall from our cell. They got to have a TV in the room along with mats, blankets, and pillows, they had the life! The woman explained that the nurse needed to come and bring the anti seizure medicine for the now pale young woman in the corner. A few minutes later she came by to say that the nurse had been alerted. Time, I couldn't judge time and the lights all on bright, how much time would it take? Why wasn't the nurse coming? The gal looked to be getting sicker, so one of the women pushed the emergency button that rang at the guard's station. The same guards who could see exactly what was happening in our little 12x12 cell on the monitor. He took his time answering and then very rudely said that the nurse had been informed and that this button was for emergencies ONLY! Just what constituted an emergency, I had no idea... wasn't this an emergency? Wasn't the health of the women gathered in this room important? Of course there was swearing, you could feel the tenseness of the room. After all, we were women and as such, we ARE the care givers, we truly wanted to help. It was a good thing she was sitting on the cement floor because she didn't have far to fall forward with her body shaking, she was seizing all right and then the vomiting...Oh my God! It reeked and of course, ever since I had given birth to my son, I gagged very easily. So there were about four of us gagging while several of the other women were working hard to make sure she didn't hit her head on the floor or wall...WHERE WAS THE NURSE. That poor young woman, what she must have endured in her lifetime and now when she needed help, there wasn't anybody coming. The woman next to THE button, of course pushed it, explained what had happened and the same voice came across and said the nurse was coming. Why did the button have to be pushed, couldn't they see at the guard's station that there was someone in trouble? A couple of women tried to clean up the vomit with the toilet paper. The room just reeked. I want to say a half hour later, the nurse came by, we were all asked to step out of the cell and line up on the wall in the hallway. The nurse went in; I didn't see what she did with the young woman. The trustee had gone in with a mop bucket and was cleaning and disinfecting the floor, walls, and of course my cement bench. We were finally let back in. The young woman was sitting in the corner, very white, very quiet. She didn't say anything and nobody asked anything. I think we were all too stunned that this had been allowed to happen. I know that I felt as if my life didn't matter to the system, whether I lived or died. I'm sure that the other women were thinking along the same lines.

I just sensed that everyone in the room was a little rattled by what we all had just witnessed and for whatever reason; I felt we needed a prayer. I asked the group if they minded if I prayed, everyone said it was ok:

"Dear Creator, we know you are looking over us tonight, we ask that you keep us safe and give us the strength for whatever is to come. Lord, we are your children and ask that you look over our loved ones; we ask that you give those in power, wisdom in their dealings with us. Amen".

I looked over at the corner and thank God, the young woman had fallen asleep. That was good. I hoped she would sleep through the night. It was getting quieter in the other cells too, so it must have been time for bed. Again: What was time?

I was back up on the cement bench in the corner, letting the wall prop me up as I must have drifted back to sleep. The women on the floor were having a talk fest; they actually seemed to be having a good time. The woman with the heart condition was feeling uncomfortable. I woke up to hear her pounding on the cell door, trying to wake the trustee or get the Matron's attention. She wanted to know when the nurse was going to bring her medicine. After a few minutes, she pushed THE button and of course the guard was not amused, told her the button was for emergencies only. She said it was an emergency, she needed her medicine! He told her the nurse would take care of it. She was afraid that she was going to have congestive heart failure due to the water build up. Oh, here we go again, I thought to myself. What will it take, does one of us have to die in order for someone to take notice. It was cold, so cold. All I could think of, was I ever going to be warm again?

I must have fallen asleep and woke to hear the keys opening the door. Next I heard "Faher!" The Matron asked me and the young woman who had been arrested on a bond violation to come out in the hall. What now? In the hall were two gray tubs with our names on them. The Matron lead us to the room that I was stripped searched in when I was booked. She told us that we were being sent up to the "floor" and needed to be dressed out. Oh My God, Oh My God, I shouldn't have to go up on the floor, I was getting out in the morning, and I was being tethered! Well, she could appreciate that, she said, but I was going to dress out and go up on the floor and that was that. We undressed, she searched both of us and finally to turn around and bend over, oh, not this again…yes, we grunted in unison. I was thankful that my bra was not an underwire, I got to keep it. I was given a red jump suit, it was obvious that it was a man's uniform, it didn't fit the female form at all. It made no allowance for hips, so to get it to go around mine; I had to have a very large size which meant it was way too long. Maybe that was a good thing, I didn't have socks and the sandals were no warmth.

She told us to pick up the gray tubs and we proceeded to a cell of our own. It was just the two of us! We looked inside the tubs and there was a gray wool blanket and a sheet! We decided to share the cement bench as a bed, both of us with our heads at different ends and the sheets and blankets covering us. This was the first time that I had been able to stretch out since my first night. We could hear the women in our old cell talking and laughing. I must have drifted back to sleep.

I was awakened by my cell mate, breakfast was here. You didn't have to tell me again. I ate the breakfast, not knowing what was next. As soon as we were done, the Matron came and got us and took us through a maze of hallways, up the elevator and finally to our "quad". The double doors were opened; we walked in and were told which new cells were ours. There must have been about fifteen women already there. My cell was on the second story on the end. I had to carry the gray tub up the stairs and at the same time, try not to trip on the pant legs that were too long and keep the sandals on my feet that were too big. There was a woman sitting on her bunk reading a Bible. I was to have the upper bunk, there was no ladder, I knew I was never going to make it. I pulled the mattress down, put it on the floor, and covered myself up with the sheet and blanket. The blanket was soft. It was new, I was told. I didn't feel like talking, I was on overload. I was supposed to get out; I just wanted to get out!

I slept and my cell mate just left me alone. I woke to hear that lunch was here. I made my way very carefully down the stairs. I wasn't hungry, but I still took my tray and my milk carton. There were picnic benches on the first floor; however, I took the tray back to the cell. Once inside the cell, I asked my cell mate if she would like my lunch. She said she would love it! She went on to say that she had lost about twenty five pounds since she had been here. That the food was not that tasty and sometimes it hadn't felt like there was enough of it. I drank my milk and went back to sleep. Time was running out, I knew that the tether office closed at two and if they couldn't get to me before that, I would have to spend another night here. Oh God I prayed, "Please don't let that happen."

"FAHER, Tether is here! Pick up your tub and come down." My cell mate asked to switch blankets, since her's was very prickly and worn thin and she also wanted my toothbrush and paste, soap, and toilet paper. I was glad that I could give it to her.

An officer escorted me back down to the holding tank. Once there I was given my clothes back to change into and my other personal belongings. After I signed that I had received everything, he lead me through a series of hallways and up the elevator to the Tether office. He ushered me to his desk, I sat down. He looked at me and started asking questions. He said that I looked familiar, and as it turned out, he attended The Chapel, the church that Miguel and I attended. He went on to say that he had been in contact with Gail and that she was waiting for me in the waiting room to be released. The way it worked was that I would have a monitoring box at home and a tether bracelet on my ankle. It would signal if I left the house. I would be allowed to leave for necessary appoints and with prior consent. He gave me paperwork about the no contact order. I was to have no contact with Miguel in person, email, phone, text, or with anyone as a go between. If I was found in violation, I would be remanded back to jail. I was given all of the instructions in writing, I would need that, I was fighting to keep my brain going, as it was. The officer put the tether on my left leg. I have to say he was a very caring individual; he wanted to make sure it wasn't too tight. There, I was done; he led me out to Gail, who had been waiting in the lobby. My Gail, my savior! We hugged, I didn't want to stop, but she wanted to get me out of there. It was January and it had been snowing while I was in the shadows of the jail. I didn't have a coat; the officer that arrested me wouldn't let me get one. It was cold, I was so cold. It was icy, Gail kept a hold of me, and she guided me to the car. I know I had a tether on, but it felt like it was:

FREEDOM!

*"This Magnificent refuge is inside you.
Enter. Shatter the darkness that shrouds
the doorway. Be bold. Be humble.
Put away the incense, and forget the
incantations they taught you.
Ask no permission from the authorities. Close
your eyes, and follow your breath, to the still
place, that leads to the invisible path, that leads
you home."*

- St. Theresa of Avila

Home at last, but not to stay

I don't recall any of the conversation on the way back to my home. When we got there, I felt like crying, but there were no tears. I was home, HOME! We went inside, I walked from room to room, petted my cat, she had missed me and I missed her. Miguel wasn't there; he must have been at work. I had the paperwork that said no contact and what that meant, I taped that on the outside door to the garage. I wanted to make sure that he wouldn't come in; I didn't want to have to go back to jail! Gail and I sat there waiting for the officer to come and set up the machine for the tether.

I wanted to take a shower and get cleaned up but I didn't know if I would have time before the officer arrived and really not sure if I was going to be needed. I brushed my teeth and took my meds for the day; hopefully there wouldn't be too much damage because I didn't get it for a couple of days. The door bell rang; the officer was there to set everything up. He put in on the desk in the den. He wasn't sure of exactly how to do it, I didn't have a land line, I only had a cell phone and luckily there was a new way of doing it for cell phone usage. He left and Gail and I just sat there and talked. Where was Miguel going to go? I wondered what kind of plans that he had made. I didn't care, it wasn't my problem! He must have known for a long time that this day was going to come.

I went to the bedroom, where I had left the lap top and gave it to Gail. I asked her to take it home, make sure everything was safe, etc. She had cleaned up after Miguel once before, she knew what to do. It was just like it was when I had first caught him cheating, using the internet, his email 'Little Black Book" had over 1000 women in it. I couldn't stand to go through it, so she went in and deleted everything for me. She took the laptop out to her car. She came inside and wanted to know if I wanted her to stay. I said no, that I thought I could take care of everything. I was a little uneasy about the possibility of Miguel coming home from work; hopefully, he would have had the sense to find other living arraignments.

I locked the garage door so that it couldn't be opened. I had locked the outside door to the garage and the inside door to the house. I sat in the den, remembering the last time I had been in there.

Oh My God, did I hear the van's door? Oh My God it was Miguel, what was he doing here? Oh My God, he had a key to the door; I had forgotten that he had a key! He was standing in the garage! Telling me to let him in! I said no way; didn't he read the NO CONTACT order? Surely the Prosecutor had told him I was being let out and that they had issued the No Contact Order. I told him I was tethered here and that he had to find another place to go. I would see to it that he got what he needed. What had he been doing for two days? Hadn't he prepared for the day I came home to my house? He said that the prosecutor told him as the injured spouse he had every right to stay in the house! I could hardly believe that, it must be another one of his lies! He was calling the Township Police. Oh My God, what next?

It felt strange seeing him through the door window...I wanted to just let him in and hug him, however, my fear of jail way out weighed that! I wanted to tell him I was sorry, that I had lost my head, and that I LOVED him with all of my being...Oh couldn't this nightmare just go away?

The police arrived; he went outside and talked to them. I wondered what he was saying. I knew they would believe everything that he said, he was so convincing. An officer came to the front door, knocked and I let him in. He said that they were calling the Judge to see what was to be done about this. BE DONE ABOUT THIS!!! THIS WAS MY HOUSE; I HAD OWNED IT SINCE 1999! He went back outside to wait for the word from the Judge. Again, here was a stranger, deciding my future. I called Gail on her cell phone and told her what was happening. I could not even think about the prospect of going back to jail, surely they would let me stay at Gail's, re tether me if that was the decision. What court in the land would put me, the homeowner, out of my own home? Miguel had never paid a thing to live here, I was supporting him!

After what seemed an eternity, the officer came back in and said the Judge couldn't be found, so I was to go back to jail, and this would be straightened out in the morning! Oh My God, Oh My God, I can't go back there! Where was the justice in this for me? It seemed like Miguel had all the rights and I had none. I called Gail to let her know that I was going back to jail and that I would call her in the morning when everything was worked out.

I showed the officer to the den so that he could unhook the tether machine. So, here we go again, the officer handcuffed me and led me outside. There was Miguel in his/my van watching as I was led back to the squad car. He sat there emotionless, Oh My God, how much more of this can I take? The ride back to the jail was quiet, I didn't say a word. I knew what the routine was now; I wasn't a newbie this time. Brain in overdrive: WHEN WAS THIS NIGHTMARE GOING TO END?

The Matron was very surprised to see me! The officer explained the situation. I sat down on the bench as my tether was cut off. It left a ring on my ankle where it had been. One of the women that I had shared the cell with saw me and told everyone, look who's back. They couldn't believe it and I couldn't believe it. The Matron led me back to the examination room. I undressed, she searched me again, and there was that grunt business. I undressed, the same clothes that I had wore in here before, the same clothes I had wore to work. I wished that I had taken that shower and changed clothes when I was home. I was fitted with another pair of sandals. I thought she would put me back in with my old cell mates, but that wasn't the case. I was put in a cell that already had two women in it.

I knew the routine, Hi, what are you in for and the same expression on their faces as I explained, attempted murder, I almost felt like it was my badge of honor. I think it was my way of saying, DON'T MESS WITH ME!

They both had mats, so they must have had a medical reason, which is the only way you got to have a mat. Here I was again, cold, tired, and still in shock over the whole situation.

The Matron came by and asked if I had eaten, since I wasn't there when dinner had been served. I told her no, that there hadn't been time and actually, I had forgotten to eat. A short time later, she came back with a brown bag and in it was a PB&J sandwich, an apple, and a cookie. I thanked her, I knew she didn't have to do that. The Trustee came to the door and asked what happened. I told her that Miguel had had me put back in jail, so that he didn't have to leave the house! As I said the words, I

23

couldn't believe it! HE HAD ME PUT BACK IN JAIL SO THAT HE DIDN'T HAVE TO FIND A PLACE TO STAY!!!

As it turned out, Monique and Littlehouse, my new cell mates were a riot...we laughed until I almost peed my panties. They were seasoned veterans at this jail business. Monique was in here for trespassing in a vacant home in Benton Harbor, yes, there was a strange story that went along with it. Littlehouse, which she said was her street name, was here for shoplifting at Lowe's. There wasn't anything little about Littlehouse, she was very short and weighed close to 300 lbs! I learned how she had made a living from shoplifting at Lowe's, but they had installed new monitoring equipment and she didn't know it. She had been caught on tape, red handed.

It must have been getting colder outside and the fact that this was the end room, made it very cold. Time has no meaning when you are in jail. The lights are never dimmed, there is no clock, and time just is. We talked for a while, and Monique suggested that if we wanted to get warm, all three of us could sleep on the floor on the mats. We laughed; I said it was like an Oreo cookie, two blacks on the outside with me in the middle. I have to say, they were very gracious to me. At one point I said to Littlehouse, I bet you never dreamed you would be sleeping with a white woman with her head on your ass, she laughed and said, I think I like it. I had to laugh at that! We knew that the only way to stay warm was for our body heat to merge. I apologized if I stunk; I hadn't had a bath and was in the same clothes for three days. They were gracious and never said a thing about it.

Sometime in the night, we got a new cell mate. She was a fairly young woman. She was dressed in her pajamas, she said she knew she was going to jail and always wore comfortable clothes when she came. She kept trying to use the phone to see if anyone could bring money in for her bail. She must have called five different people that were going to bring some in to add up to the amount that was needed. The phone in this cell didn't work as well, she had to really shout, which made the other inmates in other cells angry, so of course, there was some shouting back and forth about it.

Finally, we got some peace and quiet and hopefully would be able to go back to sleep. I was just drifting back to sleep when I heard an uproar in the next cell, my "old" home. Someone was yelling to the cell on the other side to stop kicking the wall. This went on for quite some time. I learned that the cell that had only one person in it was on a suicide watch, so she had to be alone. She evidently was laying down kicking the wall. They were keeping her down here and not sending her upstairs until they were sure she wouldn't try to harm herself.

Ah, just when you think you are going to get some sleep. The nurse called for Littlehouse, she was a diabetic and needed to have her blood sugar checked and given insulin. I guess if you are a diabetic, they don't mess around; they make sure you get medical attention.

I awoke to noise in the hallway; the trustee was pushing the cart with breakfast. I was actually hungry, scrambled eggs, toast, and juice. Back on the cement bench, again, waiting, waiting, waiting. I was hoping that someone would see the folly in making me get out of my own home! I wondered how Miguel could live with himself, putting me out of my home.

Finally, the Matron came in and took me to the booking desk, the Tether officer was there to tell me that the Judge had decided that Miguel was going to be able to stay in the house until further notice! I couldn't believe it! Has the whole world gone mad? He went on to say that he had contacted Gail for me to stay with her and she had said no! That her children were home from college and had no room! Did I have anyone else that I could call? I thought to myself, has the whole world gone mad? He said he would see what he could do. I was led back to the cell. The Trustee told me, she didn't have a good feeling about this. She was basing it on what had happened to her. She told me her story, the reason that she was here and that her boyfriend got to live in her house.

I couldn't believe it, Gail knew how awful it was in here, and I would sleep on the floor if I had to. I could feel myself shutting down. Just when I thought things couldn't be worse. What's next?

Here on the cement bench, I was contemplating my future, what future, was I in a system that didn't care, that I had never been arrested before, in a system that didn't care that I was a giver in the community, I wasn't a taker. I was a hospice volunteer; I had been a Sunday School Teacher for God's sake. I paid my taxes; I paid taxes for this very jail!

Sometime later, the Matron came and got me. The Tether officer was waiting for me at the booking desk and informed me that Gail had called back and said that she would take me in after all. Oh My God, I just cried, I think it was the first time that I had shed a tear during all of this. I was given back my belongings, signed for them and once again led upstairs to the Tether office.

Once we were there, I was escorted to the same seat I had been on yesterday. The officer explained that Gail was on her way here and that after I arrived at Gail's to call and an officer would come out to the house to hook up the system again. He further stated that I wasn't going to be charged for the hook up fee again. We went through the process of being tethered, again. The officer went on to say that Gail had been very worried about me, that I was lucky to have such a good friend.

A short time later, Gail and I were again out of the jail, and this time, not for home, but the next best thing. It had snowed during the night, it was cold and slippery. Everything looked clean, white, as if to say, life goes on.

Once inside of Gail's home, I called the phone number the officer had given me to have the monitor hooked up. Gail made some coffee and we just sat there. I looked over at her counter and she had a few bottles of wine setting on the counter, I told her to put those away, as part of my bonding out, I wasn't to be by any liquor, what a joke, liquor had nothing to do with the mess I was in. I didn't want the officer to see that and decide I couldn't be here, after all, where would I go?

The officer arrived and set up the monitoring system. She said the roads were getting bad, to be careful. That was that! I sat down and was so tired, yet I knew I wouldn't be able to sleep. Sleep had eluded me for almost two years and I couldn't even nap in the afternoon like I liked to on Fridays.

Gail had my laptop all set up at the dining room table, my new desk. I was able to sit down and email my work, that I was available via the internet. I asked my assistant if there was anything that needed my attention and asked her let our supervisor know where I was at. My clients were very important to me, they were like my family. Speaking of family, I decided that I had

26

better give my son a call. He answered rather quickly, which is a rarity with him. I told him that I was Okay and that I would explain things later, not to worry. I gave him Gail's phone number, just in case I couldn't be reached. He was glad I called. I told him not to come home, that Miguel had put me out of the house. He was stunned to say the least at hearing this. This was his family home and his own mother couldn't go there. I told him I was tired, the call was brief and that was that.

Since I could have no contact with Miguel, Gail texted him to say where I was at and at his convenience, she would like to stop by to pick up my car and would he please pack my meds, clothes, etc. She also reminded him that he was to have no contact with me, that that would violate the conditions of my bond. If there was anything he needed he could contact her or go through his lawyer. A few minutes later she received a text back saying that he would pack everything and put it into the car and it should be ready in about an hour.

Gail showed me to her daughter's room upstairs. I sat on the bed a few minutes and then asked if I could take a shower. I have never enjoyed a shower as much as I did that one. I was washing away the stink of how many days; I only wished that I could have washed away the nightmare.

Later that evening, Gail and her husband went to my house and picked up my car, with my things in the trunk. She said that Miguel didn't come to the door; they found the garage door open with the keys in the car. It didn't take them long and they returned soon with everything. They carried it all upstairs for me. Gail was helping me unpack and all at once, I froze. Miguel had packed a teddy bear that he had given me when were dating, I had named him Michael Bear. In God's name, what was he thinking? I immediately threw it on the floor. I can't believe he did that, what was the point? Gail said that he must still love me and thought he could still get me back, again. Later that night, when the house was quiet and everyone was asleep, I got up and picked up Michael Bear, hugged him tightly and crawled back into bed.

The next morning, when I got up, I made coffee and sat at my make shift desk, looking at emails from work. My supervisor, John wanted to meet with me ASAP to understand what had happened. My assistant asked a few questions about some pending work. I called and scheduled a time for John to come down and meet with me. He was about two hours away. We scheduled it for the following day. I wanted to get back to work, I needed that structure in my life, and it would be something to anchor onto. I felt so adrift, lost at sea. I felt like the next shoe was getting ready to fall. I was on pins and needles, so much so that I couldn't get very far from the bathroom.

I had notified the Tether office yesterday, before I left, that I had an appointment with my attorney at 2:00 today. I was only allowed to go somewhere with prior approval and it had to be important. I had to be home before 4:00 or the monitor would send an alert that I wasn't at Gail's home.

The roads weren't good, so Gail decided to drive me in her 4WD. It was slick outside. God, why did this have to happen and happen in the middle of winter? It seemed I was anxious about everything.

The attorney's office was just across from the jail, it made me shiver just to see the place. The office was on the second floor and we had to go up a narrow set of stairs. I needed the railing to help me; it seemed I had no energy left in me. I hadn't slept well, oh that wasn't anything new, but this was a new low. We were told to sit in the reception room, and that Mr. M. would be with us shortly.

I told Gail that I needed her in the meeting, that I needed her brain, that I didn't quite trust mine. There wasn't anything that I couldn't talk about in front of her. Mr. M. came out, introduced himself and led us back to a room with a long table and shelves of books and more books, a very lawyer looking room.

Mr. M. wanted to know how my jail time had gone, so I told him, leaving out some of the more personal details. I sat across from him at the table; he had a yellow legal pad, ready to write everything down. First off, he wanted to know what actually happened that night. He wanted to know everything from the moment I had received a message from a woman on Facebook, saying that she would like to tell me something about Miguel, up to the time of the officer handcuffing me and leading me out to the squad car.

It felt strange to relive that night all over again. I tried to just stick to the facts, leaving out the emotions. The law wasn't about emotion, it was just about facts. I could hear the words coming out of my mouth; it was almost like I was on autopilot. Gail sat next to me, just listening. It was the first time she had heard the entire story.

On the evening of January 3, 2011, I was finally checking my Facebook page and noticed that I had a message from a woman, which had been sent a few days before. I hadn't checked Facebook for a couple of days with all of the New Years festivities. In it, she said that she would like to talk to me about Miguel! Reading that message, I felt that sudden stab in the 'gut'. I knew that it wasn't going to be good. Every time a woman had contacted me about Miguel, it wasn't good news.

It was 11:00pm and I was getting ready to go to bed, but I messaged her back, that I was curious. I was amazed, she was still on line...She answered back and told me how she had fallen in Love with him, he had led her on, saying he was going to divorce me and when she pressed the issue, he broke it off. I had heard this story before, but it still cut me to the core to hear it again.

She went on to say that she checked out his story and found out that I owned our home and the condo in Florida and that I was supporting him. I could feel all of the blood drain from me...Where did she get this information, Oh my God, I felt exposed...what was going on here? She did say that she was from Dowagiac, I worked with women that lived in Dowagiac, and did she know any of them?

She went onto give me several different internet sites that he was on, what his usernames were etc. To say that I was stunned was an understatement.

I went to each of those internet sites, and was able to log on using passwords I had found when I went through this with

29

him before. I could barely read them. I was shaking; I could feel the anger rising in me. I put the laptop down and went back to the bedroom that Miguel was sleeping in and woke him up!

I led him to the laptop in the den and showed him what I found and that yet another woman had come forward and that I had had it. This was the final straw. He immediately started to yell that it wasn't true; the woman had lied and was setting him up! I had heard that one before too! I told him he wasn't important enough for someone to go to the trouble of setting him up! He grabbed the laptop and wouldn't give it back to me. I kept shouting for him to give me my laptop and to get out of the house! He started pushing me. I told him the last time he did this he bruised me and that I wouldn't put up with this. All I wanted was for him to give me the laptop, tell the truth and LEAVE! This probably went on for a few minutes.

I wanted him to know that I meant business, that I had had it. I had given him every possible chance to get healthy, to work on himself and our marriage. It was obvious to me that wasn't going to happen. I meant it this time. I felt it...I MEANT BUSINESS!

I went to the kitchen; the knife block was on the stove and pulled out the butcher knife. As I did that, I remember hearing 'Are you really going to do this?' I walked back to the den and pointed the knife at him and said "Give me the laptop, tell the truth, and get out or I am going to stab you!" I said it three times. He clutched the laptop even tighter to his chest. He told me I was crazy, none of this was true! That incensed me even more. I started thrusting the knife at the laptop, I thought he would finally get it that I meant business and no amount of sweet talk was going to change my mind. I WANTED HIM OUT OF MY HOUSE! In those few moments, I was to have no idea that my life was about to change...I stabbed his arm that was holding the laptop close and I remember him saying, "Mary you cut me!" Yes I did, and it stunned even me. Of course he was bleeding and to make matters worse, wouldn't stay still and there was blood all over the carpet and the Christmas tree that was still fully lit, waiting until January the 6th to be taken down. I continued to tell him that I wanted my laptop and for him to get out of the house! The fact is: He would have rather gotten stabbed than to ever tell me the Truth!

He ran to the bathroom and of course still bleeding and locked himself in. I was banging on the door telling him I wanted him to get OUT! I heard him talking to someone saying that I was trying to kill him! Was I? Was that what I was doing? I know I thought he deserved to be dead, but I knew that I wasn't trying to do that! My intention was to scare him to get out; he thought I was crazy, so GET OUT!!!

I must have changed my tone, calmed down and got him to open the door and come out of the bathroom. I put the knife in the sink and helped him sit down at the kitchen table and had him elevate his arm, wrapped in a towel. It was at this point that there was a knocking at the door, I opened the door, and the township police were there!

As it turned out, while Miguel was in the bathroom, he was talking to his ex wife, Lori and she called the police! An officer immediately went over to Miguel and took him into the den. I could hear them talking. The other officer had me sit down in the living room.

God, what Gail and Mr. M. must have thought of me...what did I think of me?

Mr. M. was taking notes, asking a few clarifying questions. Did I still have the Facebook messages, etc? Yes, I still had everything; thankfully, I had had Gail take the computer out of the house when I did. You would think that the events of that night would have been the worst of it, but that wasn't going to be the case. Next Mr. M. wanted me to start from the top about my marriage to Miguel. My marriage to Miguel, what a farce, what a tragedy, what a mistake.

I had "met" Miguel on Match.com in late February of 2007. I had been divorced for about three years. I actually wasn't interested in him because he was five years younger and as it turned out, had four children, age three to ten. I wasn't interested in being a step mom. We chatted on line for about a week and then started talking on the phone. It seemed we had a lot in common. But before I would meet with him, I had two questions that I felt were important to understanding if he was dating/marriage material:

> *1. What was his relationship with his mother?*
> *2. How did he feel about animals, pets in particular?*

His answers where that he and his mother had a great relationship and that they talked daily. He knew that if he or the children needed anything that she would be there. As for the animal issue he loved pets....they had had a cat when he was growing up that he was very fond of....So, he passed that test and we made a date to meet on the upcoming Wednesday at a Starbucks in South Bend. I was working in Niles at the time and it was relatively close.

I remember that day so well. I was wearing a navy blue business suit, with navy blue shoes and a maroon brocade purse. I wore pearls...Miguel was dressed in jeans and had an orange striped shirt on that reminded me of Finding Nemo...he had a beaded chocker necklace on and when he smiled at me, I melted. At 6'4" he was a commanding figure...he was in good shape and had the most remarkable brown eyes I had ever seen. We chatted for about 45 minutes...he had to be at Granger Community Church, were he was a volunteer on youth night. It was the church that he attended since his divorce. He walked me out to my car and as I tried to get in, he stopped me and kissed me...his kiss was slow and passionate. Oh My God, I needed to get away....NOW!!!! I had nearly an hour drive home and had plenty of time to think about what just transpired. When I got home, I texted him that I enjoyed meeting him and that I was looking forward to our next meeting. There was a dance that I was going to on Saturday, if he was interested. He said yes and it was a date!

Of course, I didn't tell Mr. M. all of that. Just the facts. We were married in October of 2007. Everything was going so well. In December of that year, Miguel's van was totaled in an accident. I noticed that he kept putting off getting another van. The insurance company was paying for a loaner, but that wouldn't last forever. Finally I persuaded him to meet me at a used car lot in Niles. He seemed to be very tense about the whole thing, I just wrote it off to he wasn't comfortable with the buying process. In a short time, I came to understand all too well why he was so nervous. His application for a loan had been turned down! He asked if I could co-sign, the dealer said that he couldn't co-sign with me! That if he was going to get a vehicle, it had to be in my name. When I was filling out the application, I asked the salesperson what had just happened. He said that he couldn't comment on Miguel's status due to confidentiality. I stopped writing and told him that if he wanted to sell that van to me, he would tell me. Evidently Miguel and his first wife had file bankruptcy and he had a credit score of 320!!!!! Oh My God, I had asked Miguel questions that related to finances to see if there were any issues prior to our marriage. One of those questions was, had he ever filed for bankruptcy and his answer was NO. HE HAD LIED!

After the first of the year, I noticed we were getting a lot of calls, as it turned out, it was bill collectors, and he owed about $5000 in credit card debt. These people called seven days a week. Miguel had explained that he had had to use credit when he moved out and was slowly paying it off. I had the means, so I asked him, would he like me to pay them off and he could just pay me? That way, we wouldn't have to deal with bill collectors. So that is what I did. He had already borrowed $3,000 from me prior to the marriage, to pay off, according to him back child support that he didn't owe, but the court insisted, so what was he to do. He had gotten a notice that if he didn't pay within 24 hours, he was going to jail. What was I to do, the man I loved, couldn't go to jail!

Next in April of 2008, on Easter morning, a woman showed up at our front door and as I was to find out, wanted to have breakfast with my husband! Of course he answered the door and told me she was lost. After doing a little computer "research", I discovered that Red1955 had been meeting with my husband for quite some time. She only lived about two miles away, was married and another big shocker; he had pictures of his great anatomy on the internet!

I went on to say that I had kicked Miguel out, I wasn't going to live with a cheater, my first husband was and I swore never again!!! But fate intervened, or should I say his parents.

They came to the house and asked me to give him another chance. He sat there and told all of us that he loved me so much, he would do anything to stay married, go to counseling, go to sex anonymous, anything I wanted. I adored Miguel's parent's and the fact that Dad was a retired Baptist minister held some bearing on my decision and against my better judgment said I would give him one more chance.

As part of my need to have answers, I called his first wife, Lori. She said he had cheated on her the same way, ten out of the twelve years! I was livid, why she didn't tell me, well, she said, I wouldn't have believed her, and she might have been right, I will never know. He had painted her as an insane person.

I made sure Miguel didn't have access to the computer at home, I knew that he did at work, but that wasn't anything that I could control. It was as if I thought his problem was with being unable to control himself with the computer. Later in the summer, I found phone numbers written in his wallet, so I called them, come to find out, he had joined a phone service to meet women! So his problem wasn't just with the internet. I was stunned, so I again, said to myself; it was the Sex Addiction rearing its ugly head. I called all of them and they all said that he had only talked to them, had not met them yet. Each of them said what a nice guy he had sounded like. So of course, I had to address the issue with him. He agreed to give me his phone and would only use it when I was there to hear everything. He seemed so sincere to work on

34

himself and our marriage.

That fall, we had been married just a little over one year, a woman showed up at the bank I worked at and was telling the teller that she had met the man of her dreams! Miguel…The teller then pointed to me and told her that I was his wife. I had not heard that, even though I was told later that the staff thought I was within earshot. A short time later that day, the branch manager came in to my office and asked me if I knew that my friend's husband was cheating on her, would I tell her? I said of course I would! She slowly slid a paper across the desk to me and told me to look on "Plenty of Fish"…sure enough, he was out there again.

On the way back home that evening, I stopped at the library which was on the way home and used their computer. I went to the Plenty of Fish site and sure enough, there he was. His profile was mostly him, with just a few little differences about him. But I knew when he had added that dolphins were his "animal" that was him for sure.

When I got home and confronted him with what I had just found out, he said it was a lie! That someone, again, was setting him up. He pointed out that some of the profile information was incorrect. I proceeded to tell him that the woman had given the teller her phone number to give to me so that she could verify this information. The teller had some personal reasons for getting involved. Her husband was my husband's best friend! As Miguel sat there, I called the number on my cell phone; I had to make several tries as my hands were shaking so badly. She answered the phone, I told her who I was and that I had her on speaker phone. She said OK, however, she didn't want to talk to Miguel. He was still insisting that this was all made up. The woman went on to tell me about my home in Stevensville, the hot tub I had and how great he had sounded. He is still saying that he never talked to her! I thanked her for talking with me and hung up. After a few minutes, he admitted that she had left a message at his work and he had called it back. That she must have gotten his profile from "the old days". He had an answer for everything! He admitted that he had stopped going to the Sex Anonymous class and that he would start back up again. I can't say for sure, but I probably started shutting down at that time.

Two weeks later, right before Thanksgiving, I got an email

sent to my work and home, from a woman telling me that she was after revenge, that she and Miguel had been having an affair at work and he had broke it off, only after she had broke up with her boyfriend. I forwarded this email to him at work and instantly he was phoning me. I didn't want to talk to him and didn't answer the phone. I snapped, I could feel the rage and I felt violated that someone could get my personal and work email addresses. I called the company that he worked for, asked for the IT dept. and after I was connected, wanted to know how this woman had gotten my email addresses. He asked me to send him the email, which of course, I did. The man at the other end of the phone told me he would not discuss this with me, however, he would look into it.

Evidently she had gone into Miguel's office and got on his computer and got them! As a result of my phone call, he was fired a week later. Evidently, unawares to me, he was already in hot water involving other women at work and his computer usage. He was willing to risk, a job that he had for over 21 years! What a Casanova....what a sick Bastard. How could he do this!

I can't say for sure how I got through the holidays or was even able to continue. Shock, maybe, I don't know.

As a result of being on unemployment, he got behind on his child support and of course, it was taken out of "our" tax return, which of course, was my money. The four children needed insurance, so I added him and his children to my insurance and paid for that. He "needed" to connect on the internet for unemployment and Michigan Works, we still didn't have internet at home, so he went to the library, only one quarter of a mile from home. I was nervous about that, however, he assured me that it would be for job finding only. And I BELIEVED him!

I found condoms in his wallet later that summer, he said that he had been cleaning out in the basement and found them in his things stored down there and put them in his wallet instead of putting them in the trash because he knew that I would go ballistic if I found them in the trash....I chose to believe him. He accused me of becoming paranoid, not trusting him and that I must be losing my mind, going thru his wallet, phone, etc. He went on to say that my trust issues were destroying our marriage.

After two years of being unemployed, I supported him, paid for unpaid child support, insurance and was able to get him a job at Manufacturing job through a client. That is where he was working at the time of that fateful day.

I had bought a condo in Florida and took the family there for a nice vacation, of course, paying for everything. I took him, just the two of us in November of 2010. I thought that just the two of us alone, we could work on getting 'us' back. I had no idea at that time, that there was no us and there had never been. One night I got up in the middle of the night and he was on the computer. He told me he couldn't sleep; again, I had that gut feeling, that something wasn't right. After he went to bed I looked through his phone and it was loaded with messages from other women. I was sick and getting sicker. I was shutting down and I didn't know what to do. I don't know how I got through another set of holidays, hosting his family's Christmas dinner, all the time with a smile on my face.

This of course brought me to January of 2011. What happened that fateful night when Miguel had gone to bed early so that he could get up early for his new job? I was checking on Facebook before I went to bed and that is where it all started…

As I was telling Mr. M. the story, Gail listening, I thought, I finally thought, what have I been doing? I am an intelligent woman, why have I allowed this man to use me, tear my self esteem to shreds? How sick am I? Am I crazy? It's like I had only allowed myself to see parts of the story at a time, but here it was, the whole sordid story, Mr. M. had written it down….the lies, the deceptions, the trust gone, the money. Oh thank God my mother was dead; she would have been livid and so disappointed in me.

I sat there, taking my breath, just BREATHE…silence. Finally Mr. M. said "This man is scum, you certainly gave him every option to straighten out." I guess there really wasn't anymore to be said about the matter. What was important is what was going to happen to me. Looking back, I know that at that time, I had never allowed myself to look at the whole of my marriage, only bits and pieces at a time. I must have known at some level it would be to overwhelming. Maybe there was a part of me that was afraid I was going crazy, maybe there was a part of me that knew I was in no condition to deal with all of this. My health had taken a turn for the worse; I was in a very deep dark place and now was feeling numb to the entire marriage and to the episode of that night. The one reoccurring thought was: I DON'T WANT TO GO BACK TO JAIL. What were my rights? Did I have any rights?

Mr. M. said we would file an appeal to get me back in my home. He could sense that it was vital to my mental health. He said that I should file for a divorce immediately. Next he was petitioning for all of the paperwork on the case so that we could proceed. He said it didn't look good and it would be my account against Miguel's account of the night and since he got stabbed, the court was going to give him the leverage. Along with that, I had the misfortune to draw Judge Willie, even my attorney thought that was bad luck. As we left the office, I felt as if this still couldn't be happening.

On the way home back to Gail's, we stopped at the grocery store to pick up my food and some supplies. I didn't want Gail to have to cook and clean up after me or be a financial burden. She was wheeling the cart through the aisle and to be honest, I had forgotten that I had the tether on. I noticed Gail was steering the cart at an angle, later I found out that there was an old woman that was staring at my tether, rather anxiously and Gail wanted to shield me from that. I wonder what the woman thought. I don't think I have ever seen someone out and about with a tether on.

We got back to Gail's home, safe and sound, back in time, the monitor hadn't gone off. I heated up one of my box dinners and tried to eat. How long this was going to go on, only the good Lord knew.

I hadn't slept through the night in so long; it wasn't going to be any different. When I tried to sleep I could feel tenseness, like worms crawling in my legs. Almost like electricity shooting through my legs. I couldn't turn my brain off; I couldn't remember how long I had been that way. I wondered what the women back at the jail were doing. I wondered about my cat. I couldn't turn my mind off. That had been a problem for so long and now that I was at someone else's home, it was even more obvious. All of the bedrooms were upstairs and I tried to sneak quietly downstairs. I sat in the den, everything was quiet, and all of a sudden, I could hear the local coyotes howling. It was such a mournful sound carrying across the fields on the cold, crisp night.

I am not one given to omens, but if I had been, it sure didn't sound good. They sounded so forlorn, just like me; at least I was in a warm safe place, sheltered from the storm.

I woke up the next morning and knew it was going to be a difficult day. I was going to meet with John, my manager at the financial institution that I worked for. When we met, he asked me to tell him the whole story of what happened that night. He sat there taking notes. After I was done, he said that he would give the information to Human Resources and then get back with me as to when I could get back to work. He didn't think there was going to be a problem. I was after all one of their top achievers. That was reassuring; I needed something to be focused on. My life was in turmoil, but the one thing that was a constant was my career and my family of coworkers.

The next few days are a blur…each day just like the one before. Waiting, just waiting to hear about my job and my upcoming court date. I didn't sleep well, I got up, had coffee and a fruit, sat at my make shift desk, connected with staff, family and friends and played solitaire. Solitaire has always been a way of escaping my thoughts, a way of letting my brain rest.

Mr. M. contacted me to say that my hearing was Friday at 9:00 am. I made sure to call the tether office to notify them that I would be leaving the house at 8:30 and would be in court. I wanted to go and have my nails done, the person on the other end of the phone seemed stunned that I would even ask that, I was told NO, that I could only go to necessary appointments.

Out of the blue, Gail got a text from Miguel, wondering how I was doing and how sorry he was about how everything turned out. Did I need anything? Now Gail had been patient up to this point, I guess she let him have it and if he really wanted to help me, he would leave my home and let me back in. Pure and Simple. That is what a real man would do. That's my Gail, my protector, my angel.

Later that evening, Miguel texted me, when I saw that it was him, my heart pounded, here was the man I loved and I couldn't talk to him, our marriage was over, it had to be. He went on to say that he was no longer texting Gail, that she offended him! SHE OFFENDED HIM! I texted back that there was a no contact order and that I didn't want to go back to jail. He assured me that he wasn't going to report that we had "talked" to each other. He wanted to know if he could call me. I said I would have to think about that. That night in bed, I clung to my Michael Bear. Could this marriage still be saved? What was I thinking!!!!!!!!! I had just lived through 3 years of HELL and I was contemplating such a question. I must be crazy!

Each day when I got up, I was waiting to hear from work about when I could go back. Each day, no word. I emailed John and he said to be patient and that it was a big corporation and Human Resources had not got back to him. This waiting was driving me insane, if I wasn't already. I needed good news, I needed to hear that my life still had a foundation, that being my career. I had emailed Ian several times to let him know my status, and that Gail was taking good care of me.

The night before I had to be in court the storm raged outside. I could hear the wind blowing through any crack it could find. The furnace was doing double duty. I lay there, hugging Michael Bear, crying on and off. The night was a never ending tunnel of darkness. Gail had a bookcase in the room, I looked through it and found a book by Erma Bombeck and began to read that. I found it amusing…anything to pass the time away. I noticed that I couldn't focus very long. I could only read maybe a page at a time. As morning dawned, I got up and showered, dressed and went downstairs to make my coffee and have my banana. Gail was up already and we were mostly silent in the house and on the way to the courthouse. It had snowed and drifted, Gail's husband had cleaned the driveway to make it passable for us. He was such a dear!

It was difficult to find a parking spot in the lot at the Courthouse. We walked on the icy lot and walked in, Gail and I, arm in arm. It is as if it took all my strength to make it inside. We found a bench in front of the courtroom and across from the elevators and waited for Mr. M. to arrive. We watched the people coming and going. Again, time had no value. I was numb and knew that I was numb. It was something that I had learned to do as a child when life was painful. As I was watching people, I turned and there he was, walking towards us. How fabulous he looked in his jeans and corduroy jacket. Miguel in all of this 6'4" glory, my heart was pounding and in a whisper, Gail told me not to look at him, reminding me that I was to have no contact with him. So I turned my body as if to shun him. Gail told me he got onto the elevator, and that I could turn around. Oh My God, my heart was going a mile a minute. I had made sure that our eyes had not met; I so wanted to get up and run into his arms and ask him to make this all right.

About a minute later Mr. M. arrived. He told us to go to the canteen and wait for him there, that he was going upstairs to meet with the prosecutor; he would be down after hearing what she had to say. We went to the canteen, I was so thirsty, and I got a Diet Coke from the machine. I looked around, there were a few other people in there and it appeared that they were consulting with their attorneys.

Mr. M. returned and sat down. He got out his pad of paper, pen and sighed. After speaking with the prosecutor, he said that Miguel was claiming that I had got him fired from his job, which was against the no contact order! Oh My God, what was next? He wanted to know if I had anything to do with that. I told him NO!!! I had been in jail and with Gail trying to survive this ordeal and Miguel's job was not even in my realm of thinking. That they would have to prove that, and of course they weren't going to be able to do that. I had no idea why manufacturing company had fired him. I had gotten him the job with a referral from one of my clients. He was still on his 60 day probation and that is all that I knew.

Mr. M. said they were willing to drop the felony of attempted murder to domestic violence c, which would still be a felony and I could serve a minimum of one year in prison. I remembered what my peeps in jail had said, let them think you are willing to take it to trial; they don't want that, it costs taxpayers money. I told Albert that I wasn't going to go that route. That would mean I would have a felony record, I would lose my house, my career and God only knew what else. The answer was No. He went back upstairs to talk again with the Prosecutor. That is what I was paying him for, to represent me, to do my battle for me. Gail and I sat there in silence and then I started in about Miguel's job. What was he thinking? Here I was fighting for my life and I had time to think about him and his job? He certainly was being self centered to think that he was a priority in my life, at this time. It was in my best interest that he had a job so that he could get out of my house and move on. What was he thinking?

Mr. M. came back…took his suit coat off, sat down, took out his pad and pen again. This was it, the Prosecutor was willing to drop it down to a Misdemeanor Domestic Violence/Battery. Since there had been a weapon (knife) and four stitches had been needed, this was the best she was going to do. What did that mean? I would have a choice of going before the judge today or wait a week and plead guilty to domestic violence/battery and stand before him to sentence me. Or I could say not guilty and wait until there was a trial. What would it be?

I wanted this over with, I wanted my life back! I asked him if he thought this was the best we could do. He smiled and said that it was and in light of the stabbing, he was surprised that I could get off that easily. I decided to take the "deal". This was all so new to me.…I sure was getting an education. The next decision was if I was prepared to do it today or wait until next week. I wanted it today! I wanted to know the consequences of my action today! I knew all too well that with each action/inaction there was a consequence. I was prepared to get this over and done with so I could deal with getting Miguel out of my life! Mr. M. advised me that the judge might decide to give me a few more days of jail, fine me, etc. There was no way to tell and of course I had the luck to have Judge Willie! I still chose to get it over with, today was the day.

Our experiences do not come to make us suffer. We attract what we need to grow, to awaken our spiritual nature. Whatever we attract, no matter how difficult, we need in order to grow and learn. Whatever we attract or experience, we can work through.
-Iyanla Vanzant

Back on the Cement Bench

Gail and I stood up and walked over to the courtroom. Once in the courtroom, we sat in the front row bench, I laughed to myself, in church I always wanted to sit there, to get my monies worth….hm…what did that mean for today?

I was to be the second case heard today. That must be good; the judge would be fresh and less stressed, wouldn't it?

The first case to be heard was a 65 year old woman who had left the state when she was 30 after getting a divorce and leaving her children with her mother and ex husband. The state of Michigan had brought her back from the east coast for failure to pay child support. The judge told her, women should never leave their children, she replied that she thought that they were in good hands, that she suffered from mental illness. There would be no leniency on her…he ordered her to 13 months in prison and $35,000 in restitution. She was to start her sentence as of today…she was shaking as the bailiff led her out of the courtroom. GASPS could be heard in the public seating. I looked at Gail and said I was Fucked!

My case was next and it had to be delayed for a few minutes because the Judge was in rotary with someone of the same name. The prosecutor had to go up stairs and confirm with Miguel that he had never been in rotary.

She came back and reported that no, they were not the same person. The prosecutor stood before the judge saying that the plaintiff had asked not to appear in court and that it was his wish that I didn't receive any more jail time. She went onto say that this was a serious crime and that it was her recommendation that I receive a sentence to reflect that. My peeps had been right, she was the BITCH!

I was called to stand at the podium in front of the judge. As I stood there, I could feel my knees shaking and wondered if I was shaking as bad as the poor woman before me. Mr. M., was standing next to me. The judge asked me how was I to plead. I said I was guilty of the crime that I was accused of. He went on to say to me that women can't go around stabbing their husbands and as such was sentencing me to 13 days in jail, time I had spent would be taken off. That meant that I had to spend 10 more days in jail. He went thru a check list of things like the no contact order, probation period, fine etc., he also ordered the jail time to start NOW! NOW!!!!!!!!!

I turned around to look at Gail, Mr. M. was telling me they were going to take me now, to give him my jewelry and that he would take care of the rest. What rest? It was the bailiffs turn to lead me out of the courtroom, to an officer standing by to take me back to the booking desk. I was just stunned, numb, words can't express how I felt, maybe I didn't feel anything, I do remember being very cold.

There I was sitting on the bench back at the booking desk. They had to cut off my tether; it wasn't going to be needed. I went to the strip room, was searched and of course went thru the grunt exercise...hopefully for the last time! I was given my gray tub and waited for an officer to take me up to my new cell, up on the floor. No holding tank for me this time. I wondered if I was going to be put back in the cell block I had been in before. It would be nice to see an old familiar face, the gal that had been sent up with me before.

I was led to a different Quad. My cell was again on the second floor, the last one on the end. But this time I had the room to myself. I took out the wool blanket and found that I had two of them this time. I learned later that because the jail was below a certain temperature that we were able to have two. One condition was that we couldn't wear them as coats for warmth; they had to be used in the bedding. There was no doubt about it; it was cold outside and cold in here. I could see where Jack Frost had magically left his mark on the corners of the windows. I remember thinking that I hadn't seen his handiwork since I was a child, living in a very old house. I decided that I would put my head toward the center of the room, keeping it away from the outside wall. It was still morning, so I just lay down.

I don't know how long I slept, probably until lunch time. That I was able to sleep was a gift from the Universe. Someone yelled to me to come down and get lunch. I traveled the stairs carefully, the sandals again, were too big and the red jumpsuit too long! When I was booked this time, and answered questions, I remembered to say that I was a vegetarian and of course, I had a meat meal. Great thing about being in jail, you can always trade something for something and meat was a high commodity. It was easy trading meat for veggies!

I sat at a table with a woman older than me! Everyone called her Miss Elsie. She was such a gracious woman and the only other vegetarian in the Quad. I found out that she was serving a year's sentence for manslaughter. She delivered a local newspaper and had crossed the road to deliver a paper to a mailbox, did not see the motorcyclist, hit him and he later died. She was still grief stricken over having taken a life. As the Matriarch of the group, she was given respect. We were to become friends enjoying cards and watching Dr. Oz, her favorite show. She did a lot of reading in her cell; she read the Bible and daily inspirational books.

My other table mate was a woman called Jayda. She was a beautiful, strong, black woman with her hair corn rolled. She too would be a fellow card player and TV watcher. I don't know the particulars of her case; she was in for domestic violence. I found if someone wanted to tell me their story, they would, it was theirs to speak. It actually looked like she had taken a liking to Miss Elsie, they were always together.

I learned that this quad also housed one of the ladies that I had met in the tank and now our cells were next to each other. Ms. Tabor X was in for domestic violence against her son. The night that she was arrested, she was celebrating her birthday at another son's home in a local trailer park. She had five sons and one of which she had called and told him not to come over...he always caused trouble. Well, there had been a lot of drinking, the son in question showed up and wouldn't leave and she ended up stabbing him. She was not able to make bail, so she had been here the whole time while I was out. As she put it, she got good food, a bed, TV, what more did she need. For whatever reason, we hit it off and often sat together. I laughed a lot...she had some stories to tell, I told her she should write a book, she said no, that she would leave that up to me. She asked me to change her name, which I have done! I have images of what she must have looked like the night she had been arrested and booked. She said she was drunk, had wet herself in the back of the squad car and had to be cleaned up. She had worn a blonde Tina Turner wig, a mini skirt and high boots, she must have been quite a sight.

The first couple of days were just a blur of lights on when I woke up, meal time, TV, playing cards, and lights out at 9:30. It was a time to socialize and go with the flow. The only real chore we had was to keep the Quad clean and our cells were to be neat and straightened. I was lucky that just like the time that I spent in the tank, everyone was very respectful. I believe if you give respect you usually are going to get it.

The third day started out like any other day. At about 10:00, I heard "Faher, come to the door". I made my way down the stairs. A man was there and handed me an envelope through the slot in the door. I was being served divorce papers!!! My heart rate had accelerated, that gut wrenching feeling as I read the documents and I was getting madder and madder and could feel myself shutting down. The gals asked me what I got and I told them Miguel had had divorce papers served on me. I went back to my cell and went to bed. I stayed there until dinner was served. I remember having a headache and my bones really ached. I didn't know if it was from the lack of heat or the fact that they still hadn't given me my medicine. It was interesting how the group could take on the emotion of one in the group. They all wanted to know what the documents meant. Was Miguel getting out of my house? What did he want?

In all honesty, I told them, I hadn't been able to read all of the pages. It had made me sick. By now the women in the quad knew my story and were sympathetic to this white woman that had a man that did not respect her and all he could think about was himself and my money. That pretty much summed it up. I told them that after I had read everything, I would fill them in. Several of the women had made comments over the past couple of days that since I didn't call the police on him when a month prior to all of this, he had shoved me so hard taking the computer away from me, that it had bruised my left breast. I guess there is a code on the street between a man and a woman, if you don't call the police, I won't call the police. They all said that Miguel had broken that code, especially since his cheating had started it all. I was kind of

47

in disbelief that people who lived with infidelity had a code of "honor"…it was quite amazing. So I asked why so many of the women in here were in for domestic violence and each one said, because it had escalated into a life and death situation or a neighbor had called.

Sometime later that day, I did go back up to the cell, sat down, tried to center myself and read each page….going through the legal wording of the document. I sat there just stunned! Miguel not only wanted half of everything, he wanted alimony because I had got him fired! This of course was a bunch of rot. His attorney was Peter J. Jones, who, as the document said, expected me to pay the attorney's fees!!! Miguel wanted money from my IRA and Roth IRA's that I had before we were even married. What was he thinking? The document went on to say that I was to pay all of his expenses while he lived in MY home!

I grew up with my mother always telling me if I was in trouble, the police and the law were there to help and I had always had a respect for the legal system, brought up to believe it was the best in the world. But as I sat there and remembered what my peeps had been saying, it was all too obvious to me, that it was not a just system and in fact it was the BITCH!

Of course, I didn't go into detail with the women, it was none of their business what I had or did not have…but let them know he was trying to grab everything that he could and in my opinion wasn't deserving of any of it.

I was thinking back to all of the premarital discussions we had about finances and money. We had kept our accounts separate and were to contribute equally to a joint account that all living expenses were to be paid out of. Of course that went out the window when Miguel lost his job! The only bill that he had kept up with was the van payment. In thinking about those discussions, it was apparent that he had lied about everything! I had put together a portfolio of my assets so he would know what I had and he was supposed to do the same thing. I remembered that we had even talked of me selling my home and together we would buy a home in South Bend, closer to his children and their schools. He said he had money set aside from the sale of

his home. Of course later it had come out that the house
had been lost due to the bankruptcy.
One day when I was out in the flower garden, sitting on the
cement bench, he said he knew that I loved my home and he
would be willing to drive back and forth to work, so that I
could stay here. I thought he was a Prince among men....
What little was left in his 401k after his divorce had been
used to pay off the van after the accident, the amount that
the insurance didn't cover after the accident. Miguel had
no money, he was still getting unemployment and that paid
child support and the van payment. I understood all too
well what his financial situation was and why he was
fighting so hard to get my money!

Mary A. Faher, a Financial Advisor, had not taken the time
to get a prenuptial!!! Of all of the stupid things I had done, that
just about topped it. I had thought about it, but felt like if I went
there, I was saying I wasn't sure about the marriage. What a
FOOL, what a FOOL!

Each night after lockdown and the lights were shut off, it
was much harder to shut the brain off. Between the cold, the rough
wool blankets, and usually some sort of chatter going on in the end
cell, it was always a long night. I really couldn't remember a time
when sleep had come easy to me. Shutting off my brain had
always been a hard thing to do. The Matron on duty checked each
cell with her flashlight every so many hours to make sure that we
were alive and accounted for. I was awake each night when she
would shine the light in my face, as I was usually sitting up.
Several nights she asked if I was OK and I answered "yes ma'am,
just not sleeping". It was the discussion of the women here and the
women in the tank and that the jail had several law suits because
people had died in jail from neglect and I believed that. I had
always suffered from claustrophobia and it had gotten worse as I
had gotten older, but for whatever reason, it hadn't bothered me in
there.

The next day started out like any other, breakfast, and the
shower line started. Because I wasn't eating the meat, I had traded
it for use of shampoo and conditioner. Soap, tooth brush, tooth
paste had been dispensed, so I had that. While that morning ritual

was going on, we all were cleaning not only our cells, but the common areas in the quad. I had to laugh to myself, I had a cleaning lady at home and here, again I didn't have to do much, and there were several women that were serving long sentences actually like to clean to keep busy. I was more than happy to oblige them. I still hadn't had my medication and I felt achy and so tired.

I spent a lot of time in my cell, lying down with the blanket up over my head. I was so cold, my feet were freezing. I had not worn socks to the courthouse, just knee hi nylons and I wasn't allowed to keep those. The sandals offered no warmth either.

All of a sudden, I heard Faher, Mail! I quickly sped down the stairs, as fast as I could go in those sandals and trying not to trip on the long legs of the pants. I was in line with the other gals for mail. If you were a long-timer, you got to be at the head of the line. I was a newbie and really was quite shocked that I had gotten mail. I looked at the envelope, there was no return address, the stamp had been cut off, but I recognized the handwriting, it was Miguel's. The envelope had been slit open, so I looked inside. There was a copy of the Sunday paper's crossword puzzle and a copy of a LOVE poem that Miguel had given me in a card. What in the hell was he thinking? There was a no contact order going on, yesterday he had me served divorce papers and today a LOVE poem. No wonder I was so off kilter, this is exactly what had been going on during most of the marriage. He would lie, cheat, and then do something so amazingly thoughtful! As I walked back to my cell, one of the gals yelled, that envelope sure smells good! Oh My God, I hadn't noticed, he had sprayed his cologne on it. I pressed it to my nose and yes that was Miguel. Why was he doing this to me? Of course everyone now wanted to know what was in the envelope and who sent it. They didn't seem shocked at all; I was the only one that was stunned. They all said that he wasn't ready to give up his sugar momma...

When I got back to the cell, I laid the envelope on top of the divorce papers and went back to bed. It was all too much. Even in here, he could get to me! I didn't know what to think, what did it all mean?

Before dinner, which was always a brown bag sandwich, I came out of my cell and sat down on the landing with one of the women that I had befriended, or she had befriended me, I don't remember exactly which way it was. Her name was Robin. Now, I have to admit that on the outside, she might not have been someone I would have gravitated toward. She was covered in Tattoos, including her face, her neck and plenty of places elsewhere. What I noticed first were the tattooed tears dropping from her eyes.

I learned that she was from Benton Heights, had a son and a daughter that lived with her mother, who was an alcoholic. Robin had been into drugs at an early age, to numb out. Her father had repeatedly raped her and actually had gone to jail for it and recently was released from prison. While he was there, he found the Lord and became a minister. She had looked to men, for sex to find the love that was missing in her life. She wanted better for her children, but had no idea where to start. She was afraid that after she was released that she would go back to the streets, it is all she knew. She said going back and living with her mom would drive her nuts and she didn't look forward to that. I asked if there was anywhere she could look to for help? She had been in the system so long and felt helpless. I found she was intelligent and take away the tats, was really beautiful. I felt so sorry for her. I was to hear similar stories from many others…of sexual abuse early on, of physical, psychological abuse, how can we expect people to grow up this way and then turn out "okay"?

The double door locking system was moving, someone was coming into the Quad. The Matron stepped in and ordered everyone to their cells for a lockdown. This was something new and everybody obliged without a word. After we were all in, she talked into her mike on her shoulder, yelled all clear and immediately you could hear all of the cells being locked.

She stepped aside and a young man with a tool belt stepped inside. He was working on the new visitor system being installed. Instead of going to the visitors area where you could see your visitor face to face with glass in between and using a phone, it was changing over to the visitors would sit in front of monitors in the visitors lobby and see us right here in the Quad, that way they wouldn't have to take us to the visiting area, monitor us etc. One more way to demoralize us! I lay on my cot for what seemed to be about 20 minutes and he left. So I thought it shouldn't be long until the cells would be unlocked and of course, I was wrong as usual. It was getting loud with people yelling at the cameras in the center of the room to unlock the cells, but to no avail. We probably were in lock down for about 4 hours. The nurse came by to disperse meds right before dinner and when she notice we were in lock down, she inquired if there was a reason. The guard in the tower unlocked the cells and no reason was given other than they forgot to unlock the cells. I had heard stories of how the guards like to play head games....so it was true after all!

Everyone was edgy being locked up for that long knowing that we had little time left after dinner. I played cards with Miss Elsie and Jayda. I loved to play cards and I remembered as an only child not having anyone to play with. Who could have said that 40 years later, I would be sitting in jail, playing cards and actually enjoying the game and the company!

That night was like any other...sleepless! I was awake every time the matron came in to check on me. It was someone new, so she had to ask, was I ok? Yep, I was okay...as I sat there in the quiet darkness I realized that I wasn't alone. I knew that God was sitting there with me. My entire life, he had always been there. People had come and gone in my life, but he was ALWAYS there. I felt a calmness as his LOVE poured through me... somehow, someway, I knew that I would not only survive this, but go on to THRIVE. They say there is a reason for everything and at the moment, I couldn't say what it was going to be, but I trusted God that there was and that I would be able to use this dark period in my life for the good. I knew it then and I know it now!

When I was 11 years old I was to come to know God as one of LOVE always in all ways! It was Easter time and they always show those movies about Jesus, I think it was the King of Kings, with Jeffery Hunter. I had watched the movie and was in a real emotional battle. My mother had let me sleep upstairs in the double bed, with real springs! It was a treat, in all reality; I was out of her hair! I was tossing and turning...How could they have killed our Lord who was so good and only wanted to help people? He was so LOVED by so many! Who was I, just a little girl in Benton Harbor, Michigan...I didn't have anyone LOVING

*me, what was going to happen to me? I cried long and
hard, the kind that gives you a headache.*

*I remember seeing a light blue light in the room, I
remember feeling calmness and I remember hearing: "I
will always LOVE you and be with you, you are my own!"
Now I can't say I heard that with my ears, but some way,
somehow, I heard it. I was instantly in a place of PEACE.
At that time, I interpreted it as God and I still BELIEVE
that to this day.*

It wasn't so odd that I was having a conversation with God
at let's say 3:00 in the morning, just the two of us in a jail cell on a
cot, in a very cold room. I didn't feel deserted, I didn't feel as if I
was a horrible person for stabbing Miguel, I felt like a child of God
who had been through a lot and it was going to get better. It might
get worse for a while, but it was going to get better. The Creator
knew what was in my heart and mind, knew the state of my mind
and what had taken me down this dark path.

After breakfast, I walked to the shower stall, with my white
towel, soap and shampoo from Robin that I had exchanged for
meat. Everyone said the water was cold this morning, it was
tepid....it felt good to be clean. I had to keep pushing the water
button every so often to keep it going. I wondered what the guards
in the tower room thought, watching us all parade to the shower,
some of the gals didn't care and in fact, liked giving them a
"thrill".

It was Monday night, which meant visitors! I really didn't
expect any, so few even knew that I was in here…but my name
was called. We walked single file to the holding room until it was
our turn. Robin and I just so happened to be able to go together
with a young gal named Natasha. I thought it must be Gail, but no,
it was my friend June. I didn't know how to work the phone, but
Robin helped me with that. She was visiting with her mother on
one side of me and Natasha was on the other side visiting with her
boyfriend.

I told June about receiving the divorce paperwork from
Miguel, and to let Gail know about it so that she could contact Mr.
M. I told her I hadn't had my meds, but had signed up to see the

53

doctor tomorrow. I tried to be upbeat, she looked so sad looking at me. I really don't have a clue what I looked like or how I came across. She asked me if I needed anything or money to buy anything. I told her no, that hopefully I was getting out soon. The phone was timed and when it was our turn to go, we three got up and the next three came in. Everyone was quiet going back to the quad. It just felt good to be out of there.

Back in the Quad, I sat with Robin and she talked more about her family life. She really didn't like her mother, but knew it was the place she could stay and the only person that would take care of her kids, who were old enough to get in trouble and as she put it, probably were. I thought about my son, Ian. I would never have thought that about him. I expected him to do well in life, I wanted that for him and that is how I raised him...to be self sufficient, a contributor to society, not a taker. It was obvious that as mother's, we had different agenda's for our children. It wasn't for me to judge. It was just the way it was.

The next afternoon, I was able to go to see the Doctor. We were all lead up to a holding area. The women and the men were separated. It was interesting to see the dynamics of the men and women seeing each other. Some of them seemed to know each other...I learned later that evening just what was going on for a few of them. Oh if the walls could only talk...or could they!

When it was my turn, I sat on the bed; a nurse took my temperature, asked what brought me up. I told him, I was very achy, I needed my thyroid medication, and he asked me what was the dosage....I couldn't remember, but I gave him my doctor's name and phone number. I also needed my Prozac. He took my blood pressure, said it was a little high...normally it is normal to low.

The Doctor came in, what I remember the most was he was wearing a baseball cap, with a Christian fish pin on it. However, his demeanor was cold and aloof. At no time did he ever look at me, he asked all of his questions while looking down at the pad he was writing on. He asked me if this was my first time here and I said yes...he said no, you were here last week. I was very puzzled, why ask the question? Evidently he was referring to when I was first booked and I had not requested to see him. So what was different...again, he never made eye contact with me, just kept his eyes on his paperwork and left. The nurse came back with a packet of ibuprofen and told me the meds nurse would have my medications in the morning. Did I need anything else? The whole experience was very impersonal.

At dinner I sat with Natasha. She was originally from Russia and had been adopted by American parents when she was a young teen, and they just abandoned her after a couple of years. I had never heard of such a thing. She said she had lived on the streets up in Grand Rapids. It was there that she met her boyfriend and the father of her two year old daughter. She had lived with him and his mother for a while. To support herself and her daughter, she stole whatever she could and had finally been caught in Berrien County, and that was why she was in jail here. She said she had tried to get a job, but without a diploma, and not very good English, it had been hopeless. She missed her daughter and her boyfriend and felt so lost. She had thought that coming to America was a dream-come-true. She said dreams were for other people, not her.

After dinner, I sat with Robin up on the walkway to watch TV. I told her the girls in the far inner cell were loud for quite a while after lights out last night. She laughed…Evidently, the men's quad was on the other side and they were passing notes through the wall…now, I have to admit, I thought she was lying, there would be no way…well, I was wrong. The walls were concrete blocks and the seam where the wall meets the wall, the mortar had been bored about the size of a pencil and that is where the notes went back and forth. So yes, the walls were talking. How long and how this wasn't detected I had no idea. I was surprised that no one had ratted anyone out…Robin, in fact showed me a note that one of the guys had sent her. It was on lined notebook paper and his handwriting was fairly decent for guy. He talked about wanting to meet up with her when they both got out. She asked me if I wanted to talk to anyone. I smiled and said no thank you; I surely didn't need that in my life. Now I knew what it meant when someone said "mail special delivery" as they passed by. I don't know how many were participating, but in a strange way, I think it helped with the morale!

It was strange to think that all of these women were living together and actually getting along and for the most part, very respectful of each other.

Ms. Tabor came and sat with us saying that she thought she was getting out tomorrow, that one of her son's had been able to make the bail money. She would be tethered until her court date. She was a hoot, she had some real stories to tell and she talked about bringing up seven boys all by herself. The strangest story was that she put beer in all of their baby bottles; she thought that would keep them strong, not weak and put meat on their bones. I asked her if any of them grew up with alcohol issues, she laughed and said: "who didn't?" She said she would like to meet up with me after I got out, maybe for lunch…she laughed, but I saw the truth in her eyes. Once we were out of here, we would want to put the past behind us. She told me that everyone knew who Ms. Tabor in Benton Harbor was and if I ever had trouble with a man, to get a hold of her and she would make sure it got taken care of. I think she was serious. I learned later from one of the inmates, that yes indeed, she could probably do just that.

I woke up to the smell of breakfast. It was strange that the aroma was so strong, even up on the second story. It was the one meal of the day that I made sure I didn't miss. I did miss having my two cups of coffee each morning with a banana. That all seemed like another life. There was always meat, so I got to trade for something else, usually an extra juice. I found that I really didn't have an appetite…everyone else acted like they couldn't wait until the next meal. True to the nurse's word from yesterday, the morning med. Nurse came by and I got my meds. I sure hope that I would get to feeling better physically. I took a couple of ibuprofen and went back to bed. I don't know how long I slept, when I got up, I sat on the upper deck with Robin to watch some TV. We had pulled our mattress pads out and were sitting on them with our blankets all around us…it was so cold. All of a sudden, we heard the dual door system opening and of course everyone was scrambling, we were not to have our blankets or mattress pads out of the cells. If we were caught, the entire Quad would have to suffer with a lockdown for punishment and no one wanted to be responsible for that. Just as soon as we got everything back into the cells, the doors closed. The old timers were complaining that the guards do that just to see us scramble, they get bored up in the "tower". I was to find out that this usually happened at least once a week. Nothing like rats in a maze to keep the hired help happy!

I wasn't sure when I was going to go home and I wanted to know so that I could give Gail an idea as to when to come and pick me up. I pushed the button to ask the guard to please find out when I was being released so that I could arrange for a ride and he matter- of-factly said I would know when I was being released and not a moment sooner than that! I couldn't believe my ears, how rude! I came to understand that "they" were afraid of anyone knowing routines, releases etc., they felt it made them vulnerable to....what? I knew how many days I had been sentenced and I also knew that I wouldn't serve that long. Days I had been in would be taken in account. The jail was at capacity and they let people out early.

That night when the Matron came through to check on us, I asked her if she would please find out for me when I was going to be released and she told me she would see what she could do. The next time she came through, she said that I had 2 more days and that I would be released at about 6:00 in the morning, but that could change if there was something else going on. She wouldn't be able to give me a definitive answer, no one ever got one. Finally I had some kind of closure, but closure to what? I was taking it just one hour at a time until I was released. I had not been thinking about my future. I tried to live in the moment when I wasn't sleeping. I tried not to think about the past and definitely not the future. The only thought I allowed myself was that I wanted to get back to work and in my own home, with my cat!

It felt like the day was dragging, this must be what it was like for a lot of people. I watched a lot of TV, played cards and slept. I should have been exercising; there was a gal at the end of the rows of cells who did that most of the day. She didn't have an ounce of fat on her, anywhere. I found out that she lived with a man that was 10 years younger than she was and in fact, he was at their home with her two children. Evidently, she had gone off her depression medication because she thought it made her feel drugged, she had argued with him and ended up biting his ankle when he tried to leave and of course, he called the police and here she was for domestic violence. They were originally from Chicago; he was a carpenter and was here for a few jobs. Her story was sad. There was a no contact order out...where could she

57

go when she got out, who could she call? She, like me, just wanted to go home and yet, that wasn't a possibility. She wanted to see her children, but they were with her boyfriend whom she couldn't go near.

The great thing about women is that no matter the circumstance or where we are, we want to help others. So we all put our thinking caps on. She had come to jail with no shoes and only her pajamas on and no coat. What kind of officer let her leave the house like that...oh, yeah...I had one like that too.

One of the women suggested that when she was checking out to let the Matron know. I guess there were coats and shoes that people didn't take and could be used for just this kind of case. Okay, we had that figured out; I just hoped that it was true. Now, where was she going to go, how was she going to survive when the only person that was supporting her she couldn't go anywhere near her for one year!

I didn't know what it was like outside, but I was betting it was very cold and a lot of snow. I had heard the wind howling on most nights and Jack Frost had certainly been busy on my cell windows. I hadn't seen that kind of window frost in a long time. I suggested that when she was released to walk directly to the Catholic Church across the street and pound hard on the door. Nuns lived there, they would have to hear and hopefully they could help her. That would be her plan. Why wasn't there something in place to help others who were in the same situation? I know there had to be others. I had lived in this community all of my life, saw the jail and never gave a thought to anyone that might be inside. It is like when you are married, you don't see all of the single people, people that might be alone and lonely. I certainly was given the opportunity to see and learn a lot of things...Is that what God had in mind for me when "we" went through all of this? I would have to give this some thought.

After my shower the next day, I gave Robin my left over ibuprofen and other supplies that I hadn't used, like toilet paper, etc. She still had several more months to go and was going to need the rolls. I was getting ready so that in the early morning, if I was released I could just get up and walk out. I planned on calling Gail when I was getting my personal items back at the booking desk and dressed back into my street clothing. No use calling ahead of time, I wasn't sure of anything.

It was a night like all of the rest, me awake for most of it, the Matron shining the flashlight to make sure I was alive and me just trying to stay warm. I didn't know what time it was, but I was ready when the Matron came and got me. I had my grey container all packed and as I was walking down the steps, Robin, Miss Elsie called out to me and said goodbye. And with that, I was on my way to freedom and I made a promise to myself that I would never do anything to go back again. As I heard the dual door system close, I was suddenly sorry for my sistas that were left behind. I planned on writing to Robin to stay in touch.

Once we were downstairs at the booking desk, I asked the Matron if I could use the phone to call Gail, my ride. She said it was against the rules and I would have to use the payphone, so that is what I did. I let Gail know that I was ready to be picked up and when she got there, where to park. I changed back into the clothes that I had worn to court; they were wrinkly and smelled odd. They were back in the locker room where other inmate's belongings were, so no telling what odors were mixing it up back there. I was led down the long hallway to the waiting room. It was so quiet at that time in the morning. Even as I passed the men's holding area, it was quiet. There I sat, alone, looking outside, it was still pitch black and every light was on in here and so bright. I got to see the new area for visitors with the monitors that were still being installed. I sat there a few minutes when a young man came through the door. He looked at me, nodded, pulled up his hoodie and walked out into the darkness. I could feel the cold air as the door opened and closed. My mind was as tired as I was, it wasn't racing....at that moment in time, I was just being.

I saw Gail coming through the door and got up and with that, freedom was mine. It was freedom from jail and I had no idea what was ahead of me or that it would just be another form of jail. I was glad that I had told her to park close, it had snowed, and it had snowed a lot and of course, it was COLD! We didn't talk much on the ride back to her house. Neither one of us was/is a morning person. When we got back, I headed upstairs and just dropped into "my" bed. I think I must have slept for several hours.

Whatever can be threatened, whatever can be shaken, whatever you fear cannot stand, is destined to crash. Do not go down with the ship. Let that which is destined to become the past slip away. Believe that the real you is that which beckons from the future. If it is a sadder you, it will be a wiser one. And dawn will follow the darkness sooner or later. Rebirth can never come without death.

-Robert M. Price

Freedom

That first night of FREEDOM was just like I was still in jail! I didn't sleep any better and I kept imagining the Matron coming in and checking on me. There was no doubt that the bed was softer, I was warmer, but my future wasn't any safer than it was then.

A new day!!! I quietly snuck downstairs to make my coffee, taking time to reflect and re-acclimate to my surroundings. As I sat there enjoying every sip of my coffee, I was wondering what Robin and Miss Elsie were up to. How was their day going? What were they watching on TV? It was as if my body was free, but my mind and soul were still behind bars.

There was no doubt that I was totally exhausted, but there was a lot to do. Gail had made an appointment with Mr. M. for us to go over the divorce paperwork and what it was going to take to get me back into my home. I needed to contact the financial institution and find out when I could go back to work. I needed to set up my probation officer appointments. It was January and I needed to do taxes, pay bills, just catch up on life.

First things first, I needed to contact my son and let him know that I was OK. God, what that kid must have thought of his mother!!! I had raised him to be non violent...I never allowed him to play war, have toy guns and have any of the violent games in our home and here, he had a mother who stabbed someone! HOW DOES THAT HAPPEN?

My comfort "Zone" was my "desk" at the kitchen table. I connected to the internet, my connection to the world! Checked in with my assistant to let her know I was "home". Was there anything pressing at work etc. and to let my supervisor know I available and could not wait to get back to work.

I had started working for the financial institution in January of 2004, the year I was going through my first divorce. I had been in private practice with Raymond James Financial before that and felt that I needed the security of a big firm behind me. At RJF I had learned the ropes of what it took to be a great Financial Advisor. I didn't have the stress of having to "make it" with a husband providing the insurance etc. With this new move, I would have insurance after the divorce was final and more stability.

Over the years, my coworkers at the financial institution were to become the only family I would know. My son had gone away to college, and "friends" of the first marriage had disappeared. I have always been a people person and relationships have always been important to me. I just couldn't wait to get back into the swing of the job, but let the love and support of "my family" surround me.

As I was waiting to hear from my supervisor, I let a few of my close friends know, via the internet, where I was, that I was OK....I played a lot of spider solitaire...that always helped to numb my brain, and I needed my brain numbed.

John finally called and said that he would be able to tell me when I could go back to work as soon as Human Resources would let him know. He gave me their number and told me to call, that the HR Supervisor had a few questions for me. I asked if the misdemeanor would have any effect on my license and he said absolutely not. I imagined that over the years, many other Financial Advisors had had Domestic Violence issues. I immediately called HR and talked to Darlene. I had met her last year, so I was familiar with who I was talking to. I was nervous as to what she was going to ask, she said that John had filled her in with what he knew. So that seemed easy enough. So when could I go back to work? She said that she would have to let me know after HR at the corporate office in Cincinnati, OH had made their decision! Decision, wait a minute, was there any question about me coming back to work??? She wasn't giving up any information...just that my "fate" was to be decided there!!! Oh My God, I never dreamed that I was going to lose my job!!! I knew that it would have been automatically over if I had been convicted of a felony! I also knew that a coworker had pleaded guilty to domestic violence last year and he still had his job. Of course, there was no knife involved, but still.

I can't explain how my stomach was doing butterflies; my gut was putting me on alert. If I lose this job, what am I going to do…STOP IT MARY, do not let that enter your head. You have been through enough, just BREATHE!!!

I immediately called John, my supervisor. He told me as far as he knew, it was just a formality and he hadn't been given any indication that my position was in jeopardy. He was as anxious as I was to get me back to work. I felt so much better; however, I wasn't going to totally relax on this until I was sitting behind my desk. He reminded me that I was to still stay away from the financial institution at this time, unless I was doing my own business. With my 'family' of coworkers, it was going to be hard.

I have never been much of a television watcher and Gail did not have cable. She had an antenna, which got a lot of the oldies and the major networks. I sure missed HGTV. To pass the time of day, I did a lot of crossword puzzles, spider solitaire, and watching shows that were from a much simpler time. It was almost like they were soothing me, harking back to a time that Miguel, jail, life had happened. I did notice that my attention span was very short and it was hard for me to focus.

I had Gail contact Miguel about getting all of the tax information together, so I could have Gail do our taxes. At least I could get that done. She had him leave them in a bag on the door of the house and she picked it up one night on her way to see her husband at work. That gave me something constructive to do. She had turbo tax which would make it easier. I had always done my own taxes, however, that was back when I had a brain and could concentrate. Concentration, even trying to find the correct words to speak was difficult. My brain just wasn't functioning well.

One snowy afternoon we started on the taxes. I had always kept good records so it was fairly easy to do. 2010 had been my best grossing year ever, I was glad that I could still use Miguel's two girls as our deductions. This was going to be the last year I was ever going to have to file tax returns with him again. That felt good just to think about. Last year, the IRS had kept part of my tax return for his back child support. I hoped that this year, he was being truthful when he told me it was all paid up.

The next couple of days are just a blur of not sleeping at night, getting up and making coffee, having a fruit and going on the internet to catch up. I wanted so much to email Miguel, but I knew that would violate the court order and my probation, which could mean 180 days in jail and I could not go to jail again. Jail...I wondered what my sisters were doing.

My focus was on going back to work. That was a saving "grace" for me. I had been in jail, I had lost my marriage, I was kicked out of my home, I couldn't see my cat and my heart was shredded to pieces, let alone what the toll of all of this had done to my health, physically and emotionally.

I had an appointment with Mr. M. to go over the divorce situation. Of course I took Gail with me, she was my brain. Mr. M. started by saying he was sorry that I had to serve additional jail time, he didn't think if I had had a different judge it would have gone that way. But it was over and I could move on.

He had gotten the information from Gail that Miguel had had divorce papers served on me while I was in jail. He said that it was unfortunate that Miguel beat us to that. It may have made a difference of who was living in the house.

I had not signed a prenuptial, but there is a little known Dowry Rights clause that Michigan enacted in the late 1800's that Miguel was using to his advantage. It was meant to protect women that were being divorced and had never worked outside of the home and were being supported by their spouse. Well, since I had supported Miguel for the last 2 ½ years, he was able to have 25% of what I made in the last 3 ½ years of our marriage, which just so happened to be the best earning years so far for me! Well, well, well, I not only provided him everything that he ever wanted and more, but now I was going to pay through the nose, just to get rid of him! I was sick to my stomach, again. It wasn't enough that he had already cost me money, my health, mentally and physically, when would this nightmare end. HOW COULD I HAVE BEEN SO STUPID?

Mr. M. said he was also going to work on getting me back in my home. He was going to see if there was any way to move the court date up for that. He was filing the counter divorce documents and would get back to me and reminded me once again about the no contact order for Miguel.

After we left the attorney's office, we went grocery shopping. Again, I didn't want Gail to have to worry about feeding me. It was more than enough that she was providing me with a place to stay. It was an odd feeling. I didn't have the tether on, but I felt so strange to be out and about with so many people. It actually was draining just to be where other people were. I really needed to rest so that when I went back to work, I would be at my best. I was glad to get back to my safety nest at Gail's.

Later that night, I got a text from Miguel! He was going on about how much he loved me and didn't want the divorce, that his attorney had talked him into all of that. That this is not what he wanted. He went on to say that if I responded back, he wouldn't report me to the police, for the violation of the no contact order. He also was going to do what he could to get that dropped so that I could come home. He had been busy while I was in jail, he had painted the front room with the paint I had bought before all of this mess happened. He wanted everything to be perfect for me when I got home. He went on to say that he hoped I knew that he was so in love with me, PLEASE contact him!

What was I going to do? Oh My God, how he continued to pull on my heart strings! My head told me that I was going to divorce this man; my heart and body were saying something entirely different. I knew I couldn't discuss this with Gail, she would have blown her lid, besides, I didn't need to discuss it with her, I knew where she stood, I knew where the law stood, I just didn't know where I stood. I know where I should have stood, but everything seemed so surreal, I really could sense that my brain was not functioning to capacity, yet.

There is no doubt about it, one of the main reasons that it was so hard to say no to Miguel was our sex life. It was unbelievable and that is putting it mildly. I have not had a lot of lovers, but I know what I know. From the very first night, lovemaking with Miguel was on a whole new level. It was obvious to me that he was experienced...we talked about it, and yes he was. Miguel is 5 years younger than me, not that I think his age had anything to do with it, but his stamina was unbelievable. The frequency, the passion, the variety...if I was an addict, he was my drug. He could just look at me with those beautiful brown eyes...my heart, my hormones went wild...oh yes, I was addicted.

I had to think about what course I wanted to take...if found out, the consequences could mean more jail time. What was the risk to not contacting him? That would mean I was letting the court system dictate to me when I could get back into my home, the court could become involved in my settlement...Yes, I had plenty to ponder.

Later that evening, alone in my bed, holding onto Michael Bear, I replied to Miguel's text. I had survived jail and was scared beyond anything imaginable about the no contact order. He instantly replied back that he loved me, could we work this out? Oh My God, what am I going to do? I replied back by asking if he was OK, that I was so sorry that it had escalated to that. Again, in an instant, he replied that he was fine and that he was taking good care of Tia, my cat. My heart was pounding so hard I could feel it outside of my body. What was I doing? What was I going to do?

I lived as if I was a robot on automatic control. Each day getting up, going to the computer to see if there were any emails from the financial institution. Each time I spoke to John, he assured me that it was just a matter of time before I would hear anything. My priority was getting back to work, for some normalcy to a life I had no idea how to live. It didn't take much for me to tire, still not sleeping at night and suffering anxiety at an unknown high level, when I thought about my future as a divorced woman, again, let alone if I was to be unemployed.

The phone rang, I answered it and it was a conference call with John, my supervisor and Darlene, HR at the financial institution. It was short and sweet...The institution would no longer require my services. The decision had been made in Cincinnati and I could resign or they would fire me. Of course, I chose to resign. Darlene went on to say that I would be eligible for unemployment and the company would not fight it. Because they were an at will employer, they did not need a reason to let me go and none was given.

NUMB...How did this happen? How did a top producer

lose her job because of a personal matter? HOW? What was I going to do? I really had never had to look for employment, I was usually recruited or something just fell in my lap. Oh My God...what was I going to do? What was going to happen to me, no job, not living in my own home and my health had been and was continuing to spiral downward. Again, my lifeline, Gail was there to help me file for unemployment and to take it one day at a time, one moment at a time. JUST BREATHE. I signed up for MI Works; looking for jobs...did a resume on line, a cover letter...I certainly was learning new skills.

John had gone to the institution and picked up and delivered my personal items from both of my offices to Gail's garage. It was a pile and filled up his SUV. He told me I would have to make arrangements to pick up what he couldn't fit in. The day he did this, I cried, he was tearing up and said he wished the outcome could have been different. He said that my husband was not a very nice guy...I thought that was an odd statement, but none the less, true. So, here was my institution's life, sitting in Gail's garage, to be moved to where...that was the million dollar question. Once again, my life changed in the blink of an eye, my coworkers, my family, they all were no longer mine and I didn't get to say goodbye to them or my clients. This was all way too much for me to handle, I needed to get away from myself, I could feel myself shutting down, I was not feeling too good about me and the choices I had made. But like I always said, you choose the behavior, you choose the consequences. Oh yes, I deserved the consequences and took full responsibility for my actions. I walked around in a daze, I knew that I was alive, but I had never felt deader.

I got to meet with my probation officer, she was in the Niles court, as I had requested, because I thought it would be easier with me working in Niles rather than in St. Joseph. Laughable, no job, but I would have to travel to Niles for my monthly meeting with her.

I liked her from the first meeting. I felt like she was on my "side" and would help look after me. She explained the rules of no contact, that she needed me to let her know where I was living and working. I explained to her that I was no longer at the financial institution and was actively seeking employment and that I had applied for unemployment, something I had never done before. She said a lot of times that anger management classes were often a part of the probation. After reviewing my case and listening to me, she said she would prefer that I see a therapist for my issues with Miguel and thought that I could get the help that I needed. She told me she wanted me to concentrate on getting healthy and getting my life back on track. We made the next appointment and I left. It went better than I had imagined, what I was imagining, I have no idea.

I started seeing the therapist that I had back when I was going through my first divorce. It was hard that first session describing just where I was at and that I really had screwed up. It was like I was shell shocked or so it seemed. It was encouraging to me that the probation officer didn't feel I needed the Anger Management classes, just a total tune up of my heart and brain.

It has been said that the greatest souls awaken through suffering. Darkness shows us aspects of ourselves that need work, which may not have been exposed to us if the Universe had not sent this suffering in the first place. The greatest prayer you could make would to not ask the Source or Universe to take the suffering away from you, but to instead have faith that everything that happens in your life is only happening to stimulate your spiritual evolution. Thank the Universe for sending you that suffering to help you grow and evolve. All experience is a blessing and happens for a reason, so don't be afraid to feel.

- Spirit Science and Metaphysics/Facebook

No room for you at the Inn

I tried to stay out of Gail and Don's way; I didn't want to be a burden. My anxiety was at an all time high and I didn't want to be kicked out. In fact, I had asked Gail several times if I was being a burden, was there something that I could do to make it easier on them having a house guest. I actually started to help with laundry and cleaning the house. My only life line between me and sinking to the bottom of the abyss was Gail. It was like I was waiting for the next shoe to drop, but I it never occurred to me that I would be thrown out, to fend for myself. But that is exactly what happened!

One Saturday, Gail was with Don at his place of work. It was a cold, sunny afternoon and I was suffering from a severe headache with my period going full bore. I had changed my mailing address to Gail's and was sitting at my "desk" going over bills on the computer, still in my pajamas. The door from the garage opened and in walked Reagan, Gail's daughter, Kirk, her husband and x Darcy, Gail's cousin and a guy I didn't know.

Darcy starting speaking to me and I could feel the blood drain from my face, I got that gut wrenching grab and I automatically sensed that something was wrong. The others were just staring at me. She told me that I had to get out and get out NOW, that I was coming between Gail and Don and that their marriage was in trouble due to me! WHAT!!! HOW CAN THIS BE HAPPENING TO ME? She went on to say that Gail didn't owe me anything and that Gail needed them to take care of this and they were going to do just that for her. Now I was a "this". I was to get my things and get out NOW!!! I explained that my work items in the garage wouldn't all fit into my car and she said I would have to make arrangements to pick everything up at a later time!

The room I was staying in was on the second floor. I went up the stairs, using the handrail to give me support, got dressed, packed and started carrying everything downstairs and outside to my car. The five of them just sat there and watched me. Not ONE, not one even asked if they could help me. It took about four trips to get everything and my head was POUNDING... thud, thud, thud or was that the blood rushing in my ears? I was trying very hard not to cry, holding back the tears, holding back the urge to scream. As I closed the door to the garage, I could hear they were all just talking like it was just any other day. But this was the day that I had been thrown deeper into the abyss. WHAT NOW? No place to go, no job, no husband - nothing, just the abyss. When I put the car in reverse, I knew I was pulling away from my safety net since the beginning of the year. WHAT NOW? I felt like I was free falling and there wasn't a bottom. How much can one person take and how much more was I to suffer in this life. No husband, no job, no home…yes, I did have a misdemeanor to my name, I certainly had that. HOW COULD ALL OF THIS EVER HAPPEN?

Just a few short years ago, I was on cloud nine. I had married the man of my dreams; I had a vibrant career and a son who was on his way to being a success. I had my health, I had the world, or so it seemed to me. HOW DID THIS HAPPEN? I had worked so hard after my divorce to find Mary Faher, to find out what I wanted, what I needed, where I was going. I felt as if my life had gone on to bigger and better things, that the world was my oyster. WHAT HAPPENED in such a short period of time?

How could a man that I adored, loved and trusted, be a cheater, a liar, and worst of all, missing any sense of guilt over his actions? How could he have loved and betrayed me? I just didn't understand what had happened. Maybe I was going crazy, maybe I was delusional, like he said. One thing was certain, I did not know Miguel! There was an evil that I must have missed. How could I have missed that?

As someone willing to take responsibility for myself, not blaming my parents, my past, I just couldn't see how this happened. How my life took such a u-turn. It would be a few years before any of this could and would make any sense. It would take a dedication of looking deep inside and shining the light into the darkest spots, known to me and unknown. One thing was certain, I had to be brave; this was not the time to let fear take over and paralyze me.

As I sit here today, two and a half years later, it is all crystal clear. The How, the Why and even What is no longer in question. It has taken all of my energy, my sense of self, to discover the answers that were so illusive at that dark time in my life. I have often read that out of the darkest times, the brightest light can be seen. I have to say that has been true for me. I am not the same person that sat on that cement bench; I am not the same person that fell in Love with an illusion. While my journey is far from over, I am in a place that I can call my own, that I now have clearer vision not only to what is, but what should be. It hasn't been easy, the path to Self seldom is.

After falling into the abyss, I had to fight for my sanity; I had to fight for life. I found that I couldn't and wouldn't trust myself or my decisions until I could fully understand what had driven a sane, kind, loving and compassionate woman to pick up a butcher knife and stab her husband, no matter what he had done or was doing. What drove me to the edge and over? How could I live with myself knowing I had caused harm to another, let alone to someone who I thought I loved and adored? One thing was true then, as it is today, I am Courageous! My need to know the truth, my need to be real was and is the driving force of who I am.

Today, I remember Who I Am…made from the same elements as the stars, I Am God's own. My creation was and is nothing short of a miracle. The Universe planned, watched over me, guided me, and most importantly let me know, I was and am never Alone. There were times that I asked God to come and lay with me, keep me safe, just be there with me and it was in those times, I remembered I would never be alone.

The months that followed were taken one day at a time, sometimes, second by second. I went to my x sessions with my therapist. I worked on surviving not only being homeless, jobless, mentally/physically exhausted, abandonment and of course, single again. It was a lot to work on at once, but it had to be faced and done. Each area was as important as the other. I became very reclusive, keeping all stimuli to a minimum. I could barely read two sentences and television and radio were out of the question. Any loud sound pushed my anxiety even higher.

I saw my probation officer every month and reported how everything was going. I have to say, she was such an encouragement to me. She seemed genuinely amazed that I was dealing with everything in a constructive way. I looked to her to help with dealing with Miguel who was trying very hard to get the restraining order dropped so that I could come home. He had contacted her to let her know that he wanted me to come home. She was going to put him through a few hoops first. He had to go to a 'safe house' and find out what to do to 'protect' himself from me, when we were allowed to see each other. I didn't tell her that we had been texting; I knew that she would be disappointed in me and that it was a violation of my probation. I knew all too well that if discovered, I could be sent back to jail! I was willing to face that possible outcome; however, I knew that the only way I was going to be able to go home, was to make a settlement with Miguel that let him feel better about leaving so that I could get him out of my house! He was going to have to find a place to live and enough money to keep him until he could find employment.

It was bad enough being put out of the house, but the court had ordered that I pay all the bills while he was there. Here was a man, who had never paid a dime on the house, living in it at my expense. Where was the justice in that? Nobody I talked to could believe it!

After a month of being unemployed, a company contacted me about employment and hired me! I was so excited; it was a young company interested in expanding in Southwest MI. It was going to mean long hours, a lot of work and dedication. It was a positive step in the right direction into getting my life back. Every day I had a direction, a purpose. I was gaining some of my confidence back and actually looking forward to the new day.

I went to my attorney and told him to offer Miguel money to get out of the house and start his new life. I would pay half now and the rest after the divorce was final. My attorney was not too happy to find out that I had talked to Miguel. He really would not have been happy to know that we had met to go over the details. While I was there, I told him about being put out of Gail's house and he told me that her daughter had called him to get information. He knew that something must be up, but wasn't sure what it was. Her concerns were for her mother, if it was found out that I was contacting Miguel, etc. I was stunned to say the least. How did she know that it would be safe to discuss that with my attorney?

Miguel's biggest concern was that he was flat broke, he had just taken a new job in South Bend, not making enough to pay for everything i.e.: rent, child support, food, utilities, van payment, etc. I knew that I was going to have to be creative and think clear to find a way. It was the only way to get back in my house and retain some of the money that I knew Miguel would go after with that scum bag of a lawyer that he had hired.

Most people have families that can help them out. My father died when I was eight years old and my mother died when I was thirty-six. I didn't have any sisters or brothers or anyone that I could turn to. I think that was part of my problem of not having that support system which so many people are blessed to have. Actually, Miguel's mother and father had been very supportive of us as a couple and of me. I started looking at that as a possible solution. I was in this situation because of choices I had made and I didn't try to minimize that…however, if I would have went with my intuition and kicked Miguel out when I found out about Red1955, I would not be in limbo with my life. It was Miguel's parents that had pled the case for him to get another chance to set things right. It was out of my respect and love for them that I agreed, against my gut that was screaming GET OUT! It became crystal clear to me that Miguel's dad owed me! I had let my relationship with them take precedence over good judgment.

Miguel's mother had died the year before. She was such a kind, loving woman whom I adored and loved. The fact that she had been married for over fifty-seven years to the same man was in my opinion remarkable. She told me that day, that she understood how I felt, that she too once had felt the way that I did and had to make a choice, however, with Love, Forgiveness and God, she had gone on to have a wonderful life with Daddy and with no regrets.

*That had really tipped the scale in Miguel's favor.
I don't know if they realized just how evil Miguel was,
how sick, and how it would be impossible for him to
change. I don't think they had a grasp on the situation
as it was. I know that I didn't. We were looking at it as a
man that had cheated on his wife. While we all sat there
discussing the future, Miguel was mumbling how much he
loved me and would do anything to make the marriage
work.*

*I had agreed to take him back as long as he went to Sex
Anonymous, went for counseling and stayed transparent
and faithful. I would stand behind my man for him to heal
and move forward...I can laugh at that now. If I had made
the decision to end the marriage, there would be no Cement
Bench and my life would be so different today.*

Oh yes, someone owed me big time for helping me to make
that decision. I called Daddy and told him just that! I told him that
Miguel needed to move on and an obstacle to that was where he
was going to live with so little for rent to spare. I told him that I
knew that he was no longer living in the family home, it was empty
and that he should let Miguel stay there until he could get his feet
back on the ground, after all, if not for Miguel, at least for those
four beautiful grandchildren to have some stability. I went on to
say that I needed to move forward with my life and that I couldn't
see any other way. I explained to him that as long as Miguel
stayed in my home, I couldn't! He said very little and said he
would think about it.

As it turned out, he offered Miguel to stay at the house for a
small amount of rent until he could get back on his feet since he
was starting a new job and a new life, again.

I was there the day that he moved out. I know that it was
against the restraining order, but this needed to be done. Miguel
promised that he wouldn't turn me in. We got into a discussion
about how much he loved me and as soon as the restraining order
was released that he wanted to meet and to start again. I felt that

he was trying to pressure me so I tried to leave him to his packing and he blocked my way. I could feel being anxious on high alert...I just wanted to flee. It had been a bad idea to come into the house while he was still there. As I tried to flee, he told me he would call the police on me if I didn't hear him out!!! I startcd to panic, breathing hard...I couldn't tell if he was serious or not. He told me I was making him feel threatened! Threatened of all things! I begged with him to let me pass, that he was scaring me and I couldn't take it. Finally, he stepped aside and let me out of the room.

After he was done loading the van and ready to leave, he turned around to look at me and just for one second the mask fell, I saw a very frightened little boy. I made no gesture and showed no emotion. It was done, I was done and he knew it.

As I look back at that moment in time, how foolish I was! What would make me trust him not to call? He was being such a Bully, something I hadn't sensed before, so he definitely was stepping up his attack on me. There must have been a part of him that realized that I wanted him gone and out of my life, for good. If he had thought he really had a chance with me, I don't think he would have acted that way.

Miguel moved out into the old family home which was closer to work and closer to his children. He only took what he could fill up in the van and left the rest saying he would be back for the rest. Of course, he wanted that on his terms and after a month, I decided that I would take charge.

` I called my son to come home from college for Mother's day weekend and asked him to move all of Miguel's belongings to the garage. He wasn't happy about having to come home, but he did, and got some of his buddies to help him. After it was all done, he said he was glad that he had come home and was able to help me with the job. I called Miguel to tell him that if he didn't pick his stuff up within a week, I was calling goodwill and donating it! He was livid. I watched from the door window as he came and got what he wanted and I put the rest out to the trash.

It was another step in my recovery. It was hard to see him;

my heart still ached for him. If not for the No Contact order, it would have been so easy to take him back. I am so glad that my probation officer had stuck to her guns and dragged her feet on ending the restraining order. I remember just how he looked that day, as he went out the door; he looked back, didn't say anything and left. I somehow think that he thought that I would run after him...

He continued to text me, send me emails, and occasionally call. Even though I knew that it was against the no contact order, I didn't put my foot down and say STOP. There was still that nagging feeling in me....am I doing the right thing? Had I given him every opportunity to straighten out his life? Would one more chance be all that it would take?

I had become somewhat of a hermit; I went to work and came home. I felt so drained without any outside contact and my energy was at an all time low. My computer became my ticket to the world, in particular, FACEBOOK.

I looked for all of the supportive, loving sites that helped with building self esteem, pictures and quotes...I also started my own small private group called "On The Journey." It was my way of journaling and sharing it.

I don't remember how, but I came across a group that was about relationships, the head of the group was talking about her past relationship and what the guy was like...Oh My God!!! She was describing Miguel to me! Other women in the group were describing their men and it was Miguel to me! One of her posts was so riveting for me that I printed it off and highlighted it. I couldn't believe my eyes, there were other men out there like Miguel and other women like me that had tried so hard to make a relationship work, a relationship that was doomed even before it started!!! I went on to discover a couple of other sites that were about the same thing! How could I have not known about this? How could I, 'Miss has to know about everything', not know?

All this time, I had been focusing on Miguel being a sex addict, it was all about that addiction, and it never occurred to me that it could be anything else, something even more sinister! EVIL!

Now, I know that you are saying to yourself, Okay Mary...what is it? At the time of my discovery there had not been any media about this topic, that has since changed so that you might have heard of it...Miguel is a Sociopathic/Psychopathic Narcissist and I was one of his victims/source. Now, I know, you are saying to yourself, Mary, you are not qualified to make that assessment. I LIVED IT AND I AM MAKING IT. It doesn't take a degree to know what is and what isn't.

It isn't often in life that you are able to pinpoint the exact event that made the real difference in your life, however, I am blessed to be able to say yes, and yes I can. I was at work late one night just cruising through Facebook...I enjoy looking at pictures that inspire me and somehow, someway, I ended up on a site by Kellie Hernandez...I don't remember the name of the site, she took it down a short time after I had made her acquaintance. But I do have exactly what I read! I printed it off and just couldn't believe my eyes! It was describing Miguel E X A C T L Y !!!

****

I have written down, word for word exactly what she had written. I have not changed anything:

"Recovery is lost when we continue to see the pathological as having had any "humane" or "human" hearted qualities that involve anything more than what a predator is or does, throughout the relationship. **Please pay attention to this:**

He/she was, is forever WILL BE incapable of loving you. Whatever you shared between you WAS NOT REAL. What you felt was real, whatever he/she told you, did, said, was, WAS ALL A LIE, A FAÇADE, A MANIPULATION, A MIND FUCK. In order to heal, you MUST understand this with your ENTIRE BEING. You MUST find a way to accept this and write it ALL OVER THE CORNERS OF YOUR MIND AND YOUR SOUL. If it was anything you perceived as sincere or kind, that was MANIPULATION. If you perceived their blame, projection, abuse as having ANYTHING AT ALL TO DO WITH ANYTHING YOU SAID OR DID, IT IS A LIE. This IS what they want you to do. THEY WANT YOU TO ACCEPT SHAME AND BLAME. And it's so much easier to do that, than it is to accept that this "person" FAKED an entire relationship with you to get what they wanted out of you. THAT IS ALL. NOTHING MORE.

In taking inventory of my part in my relationship with my ex, the SECOND I projected, attributed ANY scene between us, any "emotion" I perceived he was feeling, as some sort of "soul" connection, even in a sick and twisted way, I FORFEITED MY TRUE OPPORTUNITY TO LOOK AT ME AND JUST INVITIED THE BASTARD BACK INTO MY WORLD AND ACCEPTED HIS SHAME...AGAIN!

True inventory looks something like this: "I reacted to my abuser this way because_____." and/or, "I was prey for my predatory abuser because it was familiar"...

"What were the red flags about my ABUSER that I missed?"

"I stayed in the relationship because I had NO self esteem, NO boundaries, etc."

WHAT about any of that has ANYTHING to do with HIM, other than that I was PREY? When you continue to humanize your ex and the relationship, you are still hanging on to a nonexistent fantasy in your head. These people are not capable of ONE OUNCE OF AUTHENTIC, GENUINE EXCHANGE OR LOVE. IT WAS NEVER ABOUT YOU AND IT ISN'T NOW, but YOUR HEALING AND WHY, WHY, WHY you were there and WHY you stayed ARE.

The longer you hang onto a sentence, an emotion, an act of what you perceive as sincerity or love for you, or some "connection" shared, you will NOT heal from this. It's a guarantee. Absolutely.

I realize how incredibly difficult, and probably the most challenging of all, it is to understand, accept and FULLY INTEGRATE that whatever exchanges you had, WERE NOT SHARED BY THIS PERSON EVER. It was a GAME to them. Whatever PERCEIVED SUFFERING out of them was MANIPULATION. These People are EXCELLENT at the pity party. This is DRAMA they created and DRAMA you keep moving through your head like a Hollywood screen play.

STOP. THE. DRAMA.
You shared nothing but a pathological bond. That's it. A
TRAUMA BOND. I think I need to put the trauma bond signs up
again. The SICKNESS in us is our PARTICIPATION (but WHY)
and that when we were out, we LONG for it. We reminisce in a
way that makes them somehow HUMAN. If our connection to
them was not going to be a soul mate status in love, it will be a
soul mate status in sickness? Do you SEE how unhealthy that is??

Here is what is helping me tremendously: While I call him
my ex while speaking on here, in my head, this man is MY
ABUSER. HE IS MY EX PSYCHOPATH. HE USED ME.
HURT ME. MANIPULATED AND MIND FUCKED ME.
WHAT AM I "LONGING" FOR? MORE PAIN? WHERE IS
THIS COMING FROM? WHY DO I THINK I WANT MY
ABUSER BACK? WHY WOULD I WANT TO BE WITH
SOMEONE WHO IS CLEARLY MENTALLY ILL AND RISK
MY LIFE, MY HEART, MY FINANCES, MY GENTALIA TO A
PSYCHOPATH?

THAT IS WHAT IT REALLY WAS!!!

I understand how badly you want to hang onto one glimmer
of ANYTHING that remotely resembles a 'soul' connection to the
predator, but that isn't possible. It never was. People who are
capable of love, care and kindness, do not do what these people do.
This is part of the SLIME you are left with and what they HOPE
you take with you...this belief that even one second in the
relationship meant a damned thing. IT DIDN'T. IT DIDN'T.

I know how excruciating this is. I understand what a deep
and traumatizing wound it is, but unless you LET GO OF THIS
FANTASY OF SOUL CONNECTION, GOOD OR BAD - YOU
WILL NOT HEAL. And you won't get to the truth or your part in
it.

We were exploited. There wasn't anything about any of us,

and our abusers that didn't SPELL EXPLOITATION for them. NOTHING.

Sincerity, love, hope, caring, passion, predictability, kindness, compassion – all of those BEAUTIFUL things in a relationship, WERE NEVER THERE WITH THEM.

Haven't you all experienced what Natalie Lu from Baggage Reclaim call the "reset button" out of these people? You have an argument and they come back in five minutes, hours or days later and pretend nothing ever happened? That EXACT thing also occurred with any "GOOD" stuff you perceive. Most of you are out of the relationship now and while some of you are still longing, some of you are moving toward the part where you are purging your own piece of this crazy assed puzzle, THEY HAVE MOVED ON AS IF YOU DON'T EXIST. They remember NOTHING of what you "shared" GOOD OR BAD. It is as if you NEVER HAPPENED. NORMAL PEOPLE DON'T DO THAT and this is why you struggle so much. You are projecting your OWN FEELINGS and PERCEPTIONS onto this person of words, scenes that happened during the relationship that meant NOTHING to them. Please work hard on this. Replace words of connection, good or bad with REALITY. When you can really do this, you will see that every single thing they ever said, did or acted upon was for the sole purpose of EXPLOITING you. NOTHING MORE.

When you can do this, you will be in a place to look at your part in it realistically, without the shame, the massive amounts of unnecessary guilt, blame, self sabotage and incrimination. Do not take on what was NOT yours. Do not ACCEPT what was not YOURS to accept in the first place. Do not ROMANTICIZE them in the slightest. GOOD OR BAD.

My ex is an abusive psychopath. A Predator. A reptilian BRAIN. A snake. My Ex abusive psychopath, USED, MANIPULATED, EXPOITED, LIED TO ME, MIND FUCKED ME, CHEATED ON ME AND GAVE ME AN STD.

THAT was the reality as far as he is concerned.

Here is mine now: What on earth made me prey for a predator? Why was I attracted to an abuser? What in my life, in my past, needs healing, BADLY? Why didn't I have boundaries? Why didn't I have self esteem? Why did I IGNORE the red flags? Was this familiar to me? If so, WHY? How can I make sure that this NEVER, EVER happens to me again? And so on...

I'm being repetitive here. This is so important to recovery and is a pivotal point in it, because the closer you REALLY GET to pulling up YOUR CRAP, Is when your brain is going to want to mosey on back to your ABUSER and romanticize it all...

You see part of recognizing your darkness is to understand why it was there in the first place. Whatever went on in the relationship was manifesting that darkness inside of you. Ironically, this has NOTHING TO DO WITH THEM AT ALL. This will happen with each and every human being that has the GREATEST MISFORTUNE OF CROSSING THEIR PATH. They will play out the pathological crazy assed mind fuck with EVERY single victim.

You will not. Whatever you did in the relationship, from lying, to reacting, to Sexual deviancy, to physically abusing back, whatever you did in the relationship in response to the bond, you MUST FORGIVE YOURSELF. YOU MUST understand that while you were "there" in the physical sense, that when you are in a pathological, very sick relationship with a very sick human being, there is NO WAY you are not going to become sick IN IT.

The gift lies in being OUT OF IT. The gift is that you have empathy. The gift is that you no longer have to do any of those things that you did in the relationship. You must look at this REALISTICALLY so you can heal. Even if there are pieces of the "darkness" left in you after this, give yourself A BREAK and some TIME to deal with it. Whatever you did in the relationship is not because you are a bad person. It's because you were WITH a very bad person. This distinction MUST be made so you can look at your stuff without the temptation of moving into drama mode about them and that somehow this was YOUR doing. We ALL make mistakes, and as long as we are here we will continue to. We are human beings, IMPERFECT. But the difference is that we LEARN from it, GROW from it, GAIN INSIGHT FROM IT AND NEVER LET IT OR WANT IT TO HAPPEN AGAIN.

Please think about this. Turn the drama and fantasy on its head…so let's start with honesty and reality shall we?…

****

As I sit here, rereading those words, I still can feel the power that hit me like a lightning bolt out of the blue. In retrospect, it wasn't a lightning bolt, but a God thing, pure and simple. I was meant to find this on that day, at that time in my recovery. I remember sitting on the lounge sofa at the office in the dark, weeping, weeping for myself that I had gone through all of that and that by the Grace of God, I was going to recover. It was the first time that I had hope and understood the "What" I had faced. The feelings of gratitude poured over me like a spring shower on a parched earth. So much had become clear. It had felt like everyone had been speaking a foreign language and suddenly "English" was switched back on. The days that followed were filled in awe and wonder with such new information.

I felt like I was a sponge sucking up every droplet and I was going to put it to good use. I was able to 'friend' Kellie on Facebook and told her, how her courage to share had changed my life and I would be eternally grateful. I don't know what happened to her, she disappeared from my list and so did her posts. I hope and pray all is well in her world.

There was so much information, several sites that offered help and many responses from others who had gone through something similar or the exact thing. It was unbelievable. The more that I delved into it, the more I knew WHO/WHAT I had been dealing with!

The biggest realization that I had was: I AM FREE! I AM FREE! I AM FREE...at last!!!!!!!!!!!!

My knowledge on cheating husbands, sex addictions was so limited; I was so unprepared for what I actually would find out. But when you hear 'The Truth Shall Set You Free', you should believe it! With my belief that Miguel had a sex addiction, I thought dealing with it would be like that of alcoholism. I had started to go to Al Anon when I first started my probation and felt that the group was helping me to focus on me, on my recovery. It was never an attempt to understand Miguel; it was all about me now. After all, I was also an adult child of an alcoholic. Could there be a link or just a coincidence? Then to find out he is a narcissist, and then adding to that a sociopath/psychopath. Oh My God, it all made sense!

It was crystal clear to me, that I had fallen in love with an illusion. I had fallen for the mirror that was me! He had mirrored exactly what I wanted with such precision that I told everyone, that he was the man of my dreams! My wonderful, unbelievable Miguel. He was everything that I ever dreamed was possible and more!

All of this knowledge released me from ever pining away for a man that didn't exist. I had never loved Miguel, I had never met him, and I had only loved the mirror image of myself. I can't tell you how this turned such a corner in my life.

The next step was going to be able to forgive myself for such evil, outrageous behavior. I had asked God for that forgiveness and know that he has given it to me unconditionally, however, I, Mary A. Faher still had to do that! So what, that Miguel was a socio/psycho Narcissist...what did that have to do with my actions? It was important for me to understand what he was/is, however, to understand me, to love me, to go forward in life as a whole integrated human being, I needed healing for myself! After all, it is about me!

This life is my gift and it is the only thing that I have any control of. I can't waste another precious moment in the darkness.

I'm not crying because of you;
YOU'RE NOT WORTH IT.
I'm crying because my delusion
of who you were was shattered
by the truth of who you are.

Dr. Steve Maraboli

There is Life after Abuse

It has been some time since I wrote the last chapter and so much has happened...lol, yes life goes on and it is all good. Even the darkest of days can be used to learn, to grow, and share, if it will help anyone else.

When I started the book, I knew I had a story to tell; a remarkable story of survival, but how to end it was a mystery. In fact, it started as a way to tell the story of the sad treatment of myself and the other women in the jail. As the book progressed, it was to tell of living with Miguel and then to living as an abused spouse to a Sociopathic/Psychopath Narcissist. It wasn't until recently that the story that needed to be told was that of not just of surviving, but the redemption of me, the forgiveness of me and yes, the miracle of unconditional Love. The Universe has been patient and kind waiting for me to grow to Love myself! As I am able to Love myself, I am free to Love existence itself.

This book has been the JOURNEY

Today, I can tell you how grateful I am that I am FREE and that I have grown from the inside out. I have learned what had allowed me to be a victim and that if I hadn't learned that one thing, I could still become victimized. That part of my story happened years ago, in my family of origin.

I was born into a working class family with my parents the first generation born in this country. I was an only child and from the minute I was born, I wasn't good enough. My father was down at the bar bragging that I was an 8 lb. boy, when in fact, I was a 5 lb. girl! I was born almost a month early, I don't know if my mother's smoking and drinking during pregnancy had any effect on that or not.

My first real memory is when I was about three years; we were living on the farm with my grandma, my mother's mother. She had suffered several strokes and my grandfather had died and she couldn't live alone.

I am standing in the bathroom room, over the toilet watching as the blood drops dissipated in the water. I can remember the red rings that were formed, but I can't tell you how I felt, or if I felt anything at all. My lip had been split from the blow that my father had delivered earlier. As an adult I asked my mother what had precipitated that and she said that I had gone behind a door and kept saying ' some bitch' and after repeatedly told to stop, didn't. Obviously, it was a phrase that I must have heard and wanted to say.

I don't remember my mother ever being kind to me or in fact loving me. I do remember the constant rollers in my long, fine hair, after all, as a perfect daughter; it didn't do at all to have straight hair. I think my father had a 'thing' for Shirley Temple and by God, my hair had to be in ringlets! The next disgrace that I delivered my parents was that obviously I was left handed and that was not going to happen. I remember my mother telling me it was a right handed world and that is what I was to be. Even my kindergarten teacher was in on it. If she caught me using my left hand she smacked me with her pen on the top of my head. I remember that pen well...it was blue ink on one end and red on the other.

The violence that was in my home was the 'secret', never talked about. I learned early that Love has to hurt and that if you act in a certain way, maybe you could avoid some of it. I do know that as a coping mechanism, I could stand there and take it and not feel a thing. Something that I used for the birth of my son, without drugs...Oh yes, use the lessons for good that you learned.

During my therapy, my Psychiatrist told me that in his opinion, that I had been abused before I was 18 months old, due to the severe startle reflex that I suffer from, even today. My father died when I was eight years old and I was left with a mother that made it clear that I was to be

*perfect, that I was in her way to have fun and go on with
her life. Children after all are better seen than heard.*

I think it is obvious that I learned survival mechanisms that
served me well then and in my first marriage. I definitely learned
the lesson well. I was the best co-dependent you could find. On
the flip side, I am a very compassionate, kind, loving and caring
woman. The kind that takes in strays, tries to rescue everyone,
except for myself. At my core I believed everyone else deserved
that, as for myself, my life had shown me that I wasn't too worthy
of that.

I learned what had enabled me to play my part in that
dreadful night. I have always said "with all actions/inactions there
are consequences" and yes, I did and still do pay the consequences.

I have also learned that from my point of reference, I was
un-equipped to deal with a Sociopath/Psychopath, a Narcissist.
That is something that I hope I have brought to your attention so
that you won't be sitting on a cement bench in jail, one day.

There is so much information out there today to educate
us…we must be armed with truth and be able to recognize evil
when it smiles at you.

Recognize what part you might be playing in furthering the
power of a Sociopath/Psychopath Narcissist. I think of all of the
things from my youth that stand out to pave the road:

"Honey, he is mean to you because he likes you!"

Well, I certainly believed that love had to hurt and if it
didn't, it wasn't love. The last few years have taught me that I
can't give love; I can't receive love, if I don't have it for myself.
That is an ongoing project "On The Journey" for me. I work on
this every day, sometimes moment by moment. In my soul, I
know that I am LOVE and that is to be celebrated.

I try to imagine what it must be like to be loved
unconditionally for just being me. Yes, I know and feel that from
the Creator God, but here on this plane, I have never had that. It
amazes me that I have lived this long and have never experienced
Unconditional, Forever Love. So, I like to tell myself, the best is
yet to be! I have not met the Love of my life…

One of the bonuses of writing this book is that I finally understand a statement that I have heard for so long;

"Lessons in life will be repeated until they are learned."

I understand my part in drawing men to me that are emotionally unavailable and do not have my best interests at their heart. Yes Universe, I get it, I know my boundaries, and I don't need to go there again.

Where you will find me these days, is sitting on the cement bench out in the flower garden. While it may be just as hard, the views are spectacular! The breezes that waft by are just enough to rustle the leaves on the Parisian Pear tree and the bees are doing what bees do. My freedom isn't just from not sitting in a prison, my freedom is that I know who I am, a child of my most precious God who knows what my soul is here to do and that, my dear friends, is to make sure you know that whatever happens to you, you are not a prisoner of your past and that you are Loved and there isn't anything or anyone that you can't overcome.

My hope is that you have been inspired to start your own journey from this day forward…to find your soul and live the life you always dreamed of. You have always heard that it starts with just one step and that is true.

Someone asked me how I got through the darkest times and my best answer was/is to LIVE IN THE NOW. You can't change the past, so don't be a prisoner of it, hopefully you learned from it so you don't need to repeat it. Looking to the future can only cause anxiety, it hasn't happened yet and you can't possibly see all of the miracles that will come your way. LIVE IN THE NOW. Now is all you have and if you need to, stay focused second by second on the NOW. This moment is all that you have any control over. Take a breath; take another one if you need to…just breathe in the life that is yours. Don't be in a hurry; let it unfold as it will.

As someone who always felt the need to plan, look ahead to all of the possibilities, I was missing valuable information in the Now. I missed or went around red flags; they weren't a part of my plan. I understand that as a child a coping mechanism was being prepared and as a Girl Scout, I was just doing my duty…well it worked for me then but does not serve any purpose today. I am in the Now.

The truth is, we are all just walking each other home and I am Blessed to have had you along with me On The Journey.

ABOUT THE AUTHOR

Mary A. Faher currently resides on the Sunset Coast in Michigan with her dog Buddha and two cats, Tia and Lil Bob. Together they enjoy unconditional Love and living in the Now.

Mary currently has a Facebook Community called: On The Journey, a space dedicated to the Journey, Living in the Light and always seeking to promote World Peace, which starts with each individual…Her focus has been to lift each other up so that together we can make a difference.

Author Photo: Amy Witkowski
Meister - Witkowski Photography
Stevensville, Mi

Made in the USA
San Bernardino, CA
28 November 2019